THE MIGHTY
QUINN

THE MIGHTY QUINN

JIMMY QUINN, CELTIC'S FIRST GOALSCORING HERO

DAVID W. POTTER

TEMPUS

THE AUTHOR

David Potter was born of a Celtic-supporting family in 1948 in Forfar, but has spent most of his life in Kirkcaldy, having taught for thirty-two years at Glenrothes High School.

He now teaches part time at Osborne House School, Dysart, and has a wife, three grown-up children, a granddaughter and a dog. He has written ten books – seven of them on his beloved Celtic – and his other interests are drama and cricket. He is an umpire in the Scottish National Cricket League. Previous works with Tempus include: *Wee Troupie: The Story of Alec Troup, Celtic in the League Cup, Willie Maley: The Man Who Made Celtic* and *Wizards and Bravehearts: A History of the Scottish National Side*.

First published 2005

Tempus Publishing Limited
The Mill, Brimscombe Port,
Stroud, Gloucestershire, GL5 2QG
www.tempus-publishing.com

British Library Cataloguing in Publication Data.
A catalogue record for this book is available from the British Library.

ISBN 0 7524 3460 8

Typesetting and origination by Tempus Publishing Limited
Printed in Great Britain

CONTENTS

Acknowledgements   6

Preface   7

1   Quinn Nascent 1878-1900   9

2   Quinn Emerging   23

3   Quinn Breaks Through   49

4   Quinn: Villain or Victim?   63

5   Quinn Triumphant 1907/08   85

6   Quinn the Hero 1908-1910   101

7   Quinn in Decline 1910-1915   119

8   Quinn in Retirement 1915-1945   137

9   Quinn the Legend   147

ACKNOWLEDGEMENTS

This book would not have been possible without the unstinting help of many people. In the first place, credit must be given to Eugene MacBride (editor of *The Celt*) for his 'fascicles' – detailed and loving accounts of every game (including friendlies) that Celtic have ever played in. The fact that he made them available to me meant that I was spared a great deal of work.

Many thanks are also due to the staff of the Wellgate Library, Dundee and the National Library of Scotland in Edinburgh for their co-operation in my consultation of their wide collection of newspapers. The Regimental Museum of the Argyll & Sutherland Highlanders in Stirling Castle was also very helpful in providing data about the death of Jimmy's son. Tommy and Anna Bolan (Anna is Jimmy's granddaughter) were very helpful with family details.

In Croy itself, I was privileged to meet Dickie Pender and his wife, who now live in Jimmy Quinn's old house in Coronation Row. They were very helpful in providing details about Jimmy's family life and gave me an example of the sort of hospitality and courtesy that one could expect in Croy. I was privileged to meet many of them on the night that Dickie handed over the ball of the 1904 Scottish Cup final to the newly opened Miners Welfare. I was accompanied by my friend Danny Leslie from the Joseph Rafferty Celtic Supporters' Club. It was he who eventually, after an exhaustive and exhausting search, discovered the gravestone of Jimmy Quinn.

Sadly, death prevented me consulting two Croy stalwarts who might have told me a great deal about the great Jimmy. One was Mr Rafferty, whom I met only briefly, and the other was Jimmy Quinn junior, grandson of the Celtic legend. *Requiescant in pace.*

In addition, I have been given moral encouragement in times of weakness by my good friends Tom Campbell, himself the author of many Celtic books, and Craig McAughtrie, the instigator of the *Keep The Faith* website.

PREFACE

It was a cricket game in the Scottish Premier League in July 2003 at Forthill, Broughty Ferry. Forfarshire were playing Heriot's FPs of Edinburgh. The Forfarshire bowler was called Graeme Quinn (who in the winter is a lover of Dundee United). He bowled to the Edinburgh man, who dead-batted the ball and embarked on a quick and foolish single. The bowler ran forward, realised that he did not have time to pick the ball up and shy it at the stumps and decided to kick the ball at the stumps instead. The man was run out by a good yard. It was an unusual but legal way of running a batsman out, and Quinn thoroughly deserved the congratulations of his teammates.

Among the all the back-slapping and congratulations, someone said 'Good on you, Beckham'. The umpire at the far end heard this and shook his head in amazement. 'Beckham! Beckham! He's called Quinn!' The young players looked at him as if to say 'So?' It was then that the umpire realised that 100 years had passed since the glory days of Jimmy Quinn and there was a danger that very soon nobody would know who Jimmy Quinn was. The umpire then decided that his winter's task would be to write this book.

ONE
QUINN NASCENT
1878-1900

James Quinn (although his birth certificate calls him Quin) was born at 2 a.m. on 8 July 1878 at 18 Smithston Row in what was then officially called Cumbernauld, but later was given as Croy. The village of Croy barely existed then, being one of the many towns and villages that sprung up throughout Great Britain thanks to the Industrial Revolution. James was the third child of Philip and Catherine Quin, joining the family of Peter, who was four, and Mary, who was two. A third son, Philip junior, would be born a couple of years later.

Little is known of the pre-industrial history of the Croy area. Croy Hill to the north of the village was fortified by the Romans in about AD 140 after Lollius Urbicus had driven back a few Picts. It became part of the turf wall known to historians as the Antonine Wall (after the Emperor Antoninus Pius who was on the throne in Rome at the time) and certainly Croy Hill does give a good view to the north in case the barbarians were to cause more trouble. The Antonine Wall ran from the Clyde to the Forth and the railway line built in the nineteenth-century between Edinburgh and Glasgow would follow more or less the same course. It is perhaps because of such Classical links that some people have said that the inhabitants of Croy should be called Crojans. After all, those who lived in Ancient Troy were called the Trojans!

Philip and Catherine Quin (henceforward referred to as Quinn, as their name was spelled this way in later years) were illiterate Irish immigrants. Their place of birth in various census documents is quite simply given as 'Ireland'. It is important to state that the word 'illiterate' in 1878 (which necessitated the person making a mark on any important document for it to be countersigned by a literate person) was so widespread as to lack any pejorative connotation, particularly in the context of Irish immigrants – among whom illiteracy was more or less universal.

The Education (Scotland) Act was only introduced in 1872. Prior to that in Protestant Scotland, education had been patchy and fitful (although by some distance better than anywhere else in the world) and dependent on the local parish church. Church of Scotland beliefs did at least contain a nod to John Knox's idea that everyone should be able to read his own Bible. In Catholic Ireland, the situation was far worse and education was the prerogative of the priesthood and the landed gentry, with the suspicion that it suited the Establishment to keep the locals ignorant and therefore subservient. The Quinns were certainly neither clergy not gentry, so were unable to read or write.

Little is known about the Quinns other than that they were born in Ireland, possibly in County Tyrone, where the name Quinn is particularly strong, or Donegal, from whence came to Scotland most of those who fled the famine. Philip and Catherine (sometimes called Kate) are given as being thirty-three and thirty-two respectively on their marriage certificate when they were married in St Patrick's RC church, Kilsyth on 16 February 1874. Ages in illiterate folk are often guesswork, but it would seem then that they were born in the early 1840s, before the famine of 1846 and 1847, and came to Scotland in the aftermath of that terrible calamity that befell Ireland and gave a further impetus to the already significant Irish Diaspora.

The effect on Scotland of the influx of so many Irish people has now been well described, notably by John Burrowes in a recent book called *Irish* with its horrific and harrowing accounts of the voyages from Ireland to Scotland and the subsequent settlement. Scotland's economy generally boomed throughout the nineteenth century, but it could not have done so without Irish labourers. Scotland, on its part, offered tremendous opportunities to the impoverished Irish, particularly if the alternative seemed to be starvation or an even more lengthy and dangerous voyage to the United States of America.

Catherine Quinn (*nee* Docherty or Dougherty) is described in 1872 as a house maid, and Philip as a coal miner. On other documents Philip would be called an ironstone miner, and it would appear that he settled in 18 Smithston Row, Croy shortly after his marriage to Catherine. Croy, as already stated, was very small in the 1870s and owed its existence to two things. One was the opening of a railway station in 1846 to service the pre-existing Nethercroy Colliery and the other reason (a consequence of the first one) was the mines sunk by William Baird and Company at nearby Twechar about 1860, and shortly afterwards in Croy itself. Baird would find a ready supply of labour in the Irish, like the Quinns, who arrived en masse from the late 1840s onwards.

What conditions would have been like for the Irish immigrants we can only guess, for evidence in a non-literate society is scant. It would be fair to say, however, that it was a far from comfortable life for the Quinns with their young family. The miners' rows, of which Smithston Row was one, were owned by the colliery. Indeed, they were built specifically to provide accommodation for the workforce. It was an example of a 'tied house' and meant that if the miner decided to seek employment else-where, he would immediately lose his house. It was one of the subtle, but effective, methods by which Victorian capitalists, like William Baird, kept the shackles on their employees while seeming to be philanthropic by supplying a house for his workers.

Baird also employed a form of apartheid in the way that he housed his workers. Aware that the arrival of the Irish in such large numbers would be likely to cause friction among the indigenous Scottish workers, Baird set about creating an Irish colony, as it were, in Croy. To modern eyes, now that we have seen the collapse of segregation in South Africa and other parts of the world, this is perhaps abhorrent, but Baird was in no way concerned about racial miscegenation. He merely wanted peace so that he could continue to make his profits. Indeed, if Catholics were fighting Protestants, the working-class struggle against bosses and profits would be much diluted.

It is interesting to examine the effects of his policy over 100 years later. Croy remains overwhelmingly Catholic, while Kilsyth is more Protestant, but hardly overwhelmingly so. There has been religious ten-sion in the past, notably at Finger Post Corner on 12 July when the inhabitants of Croy were known to barricade the road to prevent the unwelcome incursions of the Kilsyth Orangemen. Mercifully, in recent decades, this problem has been marginalized, but as late as the 1950s children in Croy were brought up with little respect for the police, who allegedly would always back up the Orangemen against the Irish. Conversely, not a bad word would be heard about the IRA, who would be the ultimate defenders of the Irish in a domesday scenario.

In Croy, Smithston Row disappeared sometime in the 1930s, but from similar rows elsewhere, we can deduce that the house would consist of two rooms. Toilet facilities (if we can call them that) existed at the back door, and water would be found in a nearby well. It is often claimed by sympathetic apologists that the Victorian era was one of progress. We can only state that if this was progress, things must have been pretty bad before. Nor is it easy to refrain from pointing the finger of censure at men like William Baird, who clearly had the wherewithal to make life better for their workers, but singularly failed to do so.

Drumglass School (near Croy) had been opened in 1871, but it was small and run by William Baird and Company, the owners of the local mine, who would therefore be able to influence who and what was to be taught. Free universal education only came to Croy itself in 1889. The 1891 Census describes the twelve-year-old James Quinn as a 'scholar', so in this respect at least Jimmy already had an advantage over his parents, in that he would grow up able to read and write. (The word 'scholar' in Victorian English means merely a boy or girl who went to school, not someone who spends all his life studying.) A new Croy School was opened in 1903, a year after a small Roman Catholic chapel had been built to save Sunday worshippers the journey to Kilsyth.

The population of Croy, which varied between 1,000 and 2,000, was almost universally Catholic and Irish. There does not ever seem to have been a Church of Scotland in Croy, although other village amenities were beginning to spring up towards the end of the nineteenth century. For young men, however, other than the traditional 'sinful' pursuits of alcohol and sex, there seemed to be little to do other than the new Scottish craze of football.

Football and Croy took off at more or less the same time. Prior to the 1870s, football had been played on a sporadic, disorganized basis throughout Scotland, but the laws were not codified, nor was there anybody to administer the game. In 1867, the Queen's Park Football Club was founded in Glasgow. For a spell they had no-one to play against and had to confine the competition to within their own ranks with games like 'Bachelors *v*. Married Men' or 'Smokers *v*. Non-Smokers', but Queen's Park and the game in general received a major shot in the arm with the first international games between Scotland and England from 1872 onwards.

The first game was a 0-0 draw, the second was a 4-2 win for England, but after that Scotland did very well, winning four times in the 1870s and drawing another. The game of football prospered as a result, with clubs being formed all over the country. Scotland had at last found something at which she could beat the English, and although the days of Robert the Bruce, William Wallace and even Bonnie Prince Charlie were now in the distant past, the spirits of Scottish patriots often seemed to hover over the sporting field when the Saxons appeared.

There was of course a massive (and virtually unbridgeable) cultural gap between the snooty Queen's Park (who supplied the bulk of the Scottish team in the early days) and Jimmy Quinn's Croy, but the interesting thing was that football very soon began to filter down to affect and unite all social classes. As such, it was one of the very few things in Victorian Scotland that did so. Throughout Jimmy's early days in the 1880s, football was looked upon as a craze or a fad in the same way that hula hoops and Rubik's cubes would affect Scotland's children in the 1950s and 1980s respectively. The difference was that football did not go away.

A ball is a necessity for a game of football, but apart from that, one can make do for everything else. A flat piece of ground is desirable, but if you are keen enough, you can play on the side of a hill, or, near Croy, a pit bing. Goalposts are total luxuries, as are football boots, strips and referees. These factors help to explain the game's ongoing popularity even in today's Third World countries.

Thus it was that the young Jimmy Quinn, throughout the 1880s, together with his brothers and neighbours would play this current Scottish craze of football as often as he possibly could. Very soon, it was remarked upon that Jimmy, although not all that tall, was broad and tough and had no little skill at controlling and passing the ball. By the turn of the century, every village would have a football team, as Saturday afternoon was slowly being conceded by employers as a holiday (such was the influence of Victorian prosperity!). Croy Celtic had yet to be founded, but there was certainly a team called Smithston Hibernians (who had a chequered and unstable history) and another more permanent one called Smithston Albion, or as they were locally known, 'Smeeston Hibs' and 'Smeeston Albun'.

There was of course an Irish dimension to all this growth in Scottish football. Many Irish teams appeared, with names like Shotts Shamrock,

Dundee Harp, Kilsyth Emmett (who also had a cricket team in the summer and included in their ranks a youngster called Tommy McAteer who would one day join Quinn at Celtic) and, of course, the famous Edinburgh Hibernians, after whom Smithston Hibernians had named themselves.

Young Jimmy would have been aware that most attention in Croy was being paid to a team called the Glasgow Celtic. They were a new side, but almost immediately after their foundation, they experienced great success. In 1892, they had built themselves a massive new ground and persuaded an ex-Fenian patriot called Michael Davitt to plant shamrocks on the middle of it. A few weeks after that, Jimmy (who was not yet fourteen years old) was aware of drinking, singing and dancing among the men of Croy one Saturday night in April, for the great Celtic team had beaten Queen's Park to win the Scottish Cup. Everyone talked about someone called Sandy McMahon.

Jimmy's father Philip was a little perplexed by all this. He couldn't really understand what the fuss was about, for the game had never really been played in Ireland when he was young, but was very aware that if this game could make so many people happy, then it must be a good thing. He saw many men from the village taking a train to Glasgow to watch the Celtic – or as some persisted in calling them, the Keltic. He decided that one day, when he could afford it, he would take his sons Peter, Jimmy and young Philip on the train to Glasgow to see this mighty team. Work in the pits now stopped at midday on a Saturday, and there was therefore the possibility that they could do this.

Philip liked Scotland, but hated coal mining. Long before his fortieth birthday, he was aware that he suffered from pains in his back and legs as a result of long hours spent underground. The Fife poet Joe Corrie sums up coalmining thus:

> Crawlin aboot like a snail in the mud.
> Covered wi' clammy blae
> Me, in the image of God
> Jings, but it's laughable tae!

Philip would have had a terrible cough in winter and sometimes it would not even improve in summer, thanks to all that coal dust. Coal mining, however, was an essential job in Scotland, and it paid enough for his family to live off. Indeed, for an illiterate Irish immigrant, there were few other options. He knew that his boys would always have a job down the pits, for Scotland seemed to need loads and loads of coal to keep all the fires going in the factories, furnaces and forges of Glasgow, where all the ships were built.

Mining, for all that it was a terrible, unhealthy and dangerous job, paid more than most manual industries. Profits were huge and the coal mine owners could afford to pay a reasonable amount to deter their workers from looking elsewhere. Industrial action and labour unrest in the coal industry in Victorian Scotland certainly did occur, but it was usually of a sporadic nature or resulting from some local grievance. Concerted national strikes in the coalfields were very much a twentieth-century phenomenon – most notably occurring in 1921, 1926, 1972, 1974 and 1984. Nothing on that scale happened in Victorian Scotland – a curious fact, considering that conditions must have been far worse, but perhaps reflecting the truism that if you have not experienced anything better, you will accept what you have.

Ireland was now a distant memory. Philip would no doubt intend to go back some day, (and he was aware that some people in the village had taken advantage of the cheap 8 shilling return by steerage from Glasgow to Dublin on the *Duke of Rothesay* every July), but memories were not fond ones. People starving to death, rent collectors shouting at his mother, that long wait for a boat, the horrendous crossing in jam-packed conditions – these were not happy events. Better Scotland with all its hard work and industry, but also its beautiful scenery and lovely music. He had heard men singing Scottish songs written by Robbie Burns, and they were beautiful, just like the Irish ones. The boys were Scottish born and proud of it, but Philip and Catherine were not really in an alien land in Croy. Everyone was Irish, and 'dual nationality' was the order of the day.

There were, of course, those who did not like the Irish. In Kilsyth, for example, some of the Ulster Protestant immigrants had made common cause with the local indigenous bigots to organize Orange Walks and other things on 12 July, so much so that on that date children were not encouraged to leave Croy. In fact, as we have seen, a 'picket' was set up at the entrance to Croy on the Kilsyth road, at a place called Finger Post Corner to discourage any Orangemen who wished to cause trouble from entering the village. Occasionally, the road was actually barricaded in a way that students of Scottish history will find hard to parallel. But apart from that seasonal activity, Croy was left to itself. Everyone knew, however, that there were often advertisements in shop windows in Glasgow for staff with the warning 'No Catholic Need Apply'. Not that this would concern Philip, however, for he was seldom in Glasgow and couldn't read anyway!

The boys, of course, had an advantage in that they could read and write. Philip and Catherine tried to learn, but they were too old and set in their ways to make any real progress. Catherine could read a few shop signs and could tell by looking at a board whether there were potatoes in the shop or not, but they could now rely on the boys. As soon as the boys reached their thirteenth birthday, they left school and went down the pits. Old Philip was quite happy about this, for it brought in more money. He had been shrewd enough to keep his head down and not cause trouble, knowing full well that this would guarantee him a livelihood. William Baird needed miners just as much as miners needed William Baird. Wages in fact were better than many men earned in Glasgow – the only problem was that it was such a desperately dirty, unhealthy and dangerous job. No major accident had occurred in Philip's time in the Gartshore pits… but you never could tell when something would happen. There had been a horrible incident in High Blantyre in 1877, when 207 men and boys had lost their lives.

If only there was another way for the boys to earn their living without moving to a big city in England or America. One of the boys told him that you could earn a living by being a professional football player. Philip laughed at the thought that you could get paid for kicking a ball, but he had heard from other sources that it was true and that this Celtic team that they all talked about in Glasgow paid their players good money. There was something that old Philip liked about that name – Celtic. Whether one pronounced it 'Keltic' or 'Seltic', it did symbolise the joining of two nations. Unlike Edinburgh's Hibernians, who were exclusively for young Irishmen, the Celtic team, under the wise management of visionaries like Willie Maley and James Kelly, made a point of not excluding Scottish or English Protestants.

By the late 1890s old Philip would find himself a fairly frequent attender across the road from his house where Smithston Albion played. He probably felt he ought to go, because he now had three sons playing for them.

Peter, sometimes called 'Pintie', and Philip were the two full-backs, both of them being able to play at either side, and Jimmy was the left winger, although he could sometimes play in the centre. Young Philip could also play in the goal.

The team played in the Dumbartonshire League against such teams as Kirkintilloch Rob Roy and Kilsyth Emmett, and in the Midland League against teams from further away like Broxburn and Harthill. These games were usually tough with loads of injuries. Old Philip was aware that his two full-back sons could dish it out when necessary. There is also a story on record of how, against Harthill one day, Jimmy got himself involved in fisticuffs with a player called George Brown, nicknamed 'Baker'. Details are sparse, but it is known that Mr Brown wandered around Harthill for the rest of his life minus two front teeth, and even boasted about this fact when Jimmy Quinn became famous.

Normally, Jimmy was too fast for his opponents. He was stocky, and his ability to swivel his shoulders often made it seem as if his opponents bounced off him. He wasn't always lucky, however, and in later years he would boast, with a touch of rhetorical hyperbole perhaps, that he used to continue playing even though he could feel the blood trickling down into his boots – but that never stopped him. He was also a quick learner in the tough school of Scottish Junior Football. There had been a great improvement in his play since he started, and Jimmy was nothing if not determined. Jimmy was once or twice asked to play for the Dumbartonshire County side against Ayrshire, Stirlingshire and Lanarkshire.

The *Kilsyth Chronicle* of 17 February 1900 lists the Dumbartonshire team for the game against Ayrshire and includes 'J. Queen [sic] of Smithstone [sic] Albion'. It was in the spring and summer of 1900 that Jimmy began to be noticed. Smithston Albion played in the final of the Dumbartonshire Junior Cup. They lost but felt aggrieved in that their opponents had fielded an illegal player. Nevertheless, the Albion made up for it by winning the Midland League.

They confirmed this on 5 May 1900, when they beat Kilsyth Emmett 6-0 with a team of: Edmonds; Philip Quinn and Peter Quinn; Hattie, Crainie and Watters; Johnstone, Mulholland, Beattie, Meechan and James Quinn. Jimmy scored once and was instrumental in several other goals for the triumphant Smithston side. Two weeks later, Jimmy was in the Dumbartonshire side that beat Stirlingshire 2-1, and the *Kirkintilloch Gazette* notes that 'Jas. [sic] Quinn was the pick of the forwards'.

The new 1900/01 season got off to a great start. For a pre-season friendly the great Glasgow Celtic sent a reserve team to play the locals and were on the receiving end of a severe beating. It was this encounter that first attracted the attention of Celtic to Jimmy Quinn. Croy was also uplifted by the news that a neighbour of the Quinns, a man called Tommy McAteer who played for Kilsyth Emmett at both football and cricket, joined Bolton Wanderers to play professional football. Some thought that he was mad, but others, including Jimmy, were curious about it all. McAteer and Jimmy Quinn would of course meet again some ten years later.

It was Smithston Albion who were the talk of the town. At the beginning of the season, at a soiree organized by the club, the players were presented with their medals for the previous season's Midland Junior League and the leader writer of the *Kirkintilloch Gazette* is writing with tongue in cheek, one feels, when he states that 'the base metal known as silver' had to be used for these medals as funds did not allow for gold!

The team waltzed through August and September, beating teams like Belhaven Athletic, Cambuslang Rangers, both the Kirkintilloch teams, Rob Roy and Harp, Dunipace Juniors and even the great Duntocher Hibs in the Scottish Junior Cup. This game was on 20 October 1900, and Jimmy Quinn, playing in the centre instead of his normal left wing, scored a hat-trick.

In the wake of this famous result, reports on the prowess of this young man kept reaching Willie Maley of Glasgow Celtic. Maley was embarking on a youth policy with Celtic, realising that the great players of the 1890s had done well, but were ageing and that new blood was required. Maley had been appointed as secretary-manager of Glasgow Celtic in 1897, with the specific remit of making them the best team in Great Britain. He set about this task with great relish. His wide network of spies gave consistently good reports of this Smithston Albion player, and Maley was aware that he would need to act quickly and discreetly.

Maley decided to see the young man in person. He chose to leave Celtic in the hands of director James Kelly for their game against Kilmarnock on 27 October 1900 and go to see Stenhousemuir Hearts *v.* Smithston Albion instead. The lunchtime train to Edinburgh was full, but he immediately recognised his old friend William Wilton, the manager of the Rangers. Fearing that Rangers too might be interested in Quinn, Maley asked Wilton politely where he was going. Wilton said he was going to

Bainsford to watch East Stirlingshire. Maley lied and said that he was going there as well, not wanting his rivals to know that he was going to Stenhousemuir to see Quinn.

The two men went to Bainsford to watch a dreadful game in the pouring rain. At half-time, Maley told Wilton that he had seen enough of this game in the inclement weather and that he was going to look up an old friend in the area. This was in fact true, but what he did not tell Wilton was that his old friend (whom he knew from his cycling days) had a horse and trap and would be prevailed upon by Maley to take him to Stenhousemuir in time to see the second half of Quinn's game!

But this subterfuge did not work. Shortly before Maley's arrival, Jimmy Quinn was escorted off with a sprained knee. Maley, however, was able to meet him in the hotel that was being used as a dressing room. Quinn knew who he was – indeed he was in awe of him and his great reputation – and Maley, on a whim, half-heartedly offered Quinn terms for Celtic. Quinn turned them down, making a joke about being injured. Maley, however, would try again, for he had liked the demeanour and the physique of this young man and knew that all his spies (shrewd judges in many cases) were not likely to be entirely wrong.

Circumstances now intervened, however, and Quinn's injury had time to recover. The game at Stenhousemuir, a Scottish Junior Cup game, had been drawn and the replay was scheduled at Smithston the following Saturday, 3 November. Stenhousemuir Hearts did not turn up, nor did they appear the following week when Smithston were again waiting for them! Why they didn't attend the fixture, no-one knows, but they forfeited the tie and had to pay 20 shillings to the Albion as compensation.

This was all very frustrating, but Smithston then played a friendly against a team called Chryston Athletic, whom they outclassed 13-0 with Quinn absolutely rampant on the left wing, and then there was a return to Stenhousemuir on 24 November 1900 in the Scottish Cup to play a team called Vale of Carron. This was a tough game, but the Albion edged it 2-1.

On 1 December, Smithston Albion defeated Broxburn Athletic 3-0 in the sleet and rain. Quinn scored the first goal 'misleading goalkeeper Fairlie with a fine drive' and co-operated in the other two. The *Kirkintilloch Gazette* also notes that 'agents were much in evidence' and that 'at least five clubs were angling for him', mentioning Hibs, Partick

Thistle and Sunderland. Celtic were not officially yet in the frame apparently; Partick Thistle offered him £3 10 shillings and a bonus, and Hibs were equally generous.

Sunderland actually offered him better terms. In those days, Sunderland were full of Scottish players and indeed were very successful – in fact arguably the most successful team in Britain of the past decade. They had three times won the English League in the 1890s and were seldom out of the top three. They had a large support and loads of money, the 1890s being the heyday of Wearside. The terms offered were good ones, and Jimmy referred the matter to his parents and brothers for discussion.

Jimmy himself was hesitant, and eventually turned down the offer for the reason that he feared he might be homesick. He had seldom been out of Croy in his life, and Sunderland was like the other side of the planet. The Sunderland representative tried hard, told Quinn about the good railway links between Sunderland and Scotland and reminded him of Scotsmen like international goalkeeper Ned Doig from Arbroath who had done well at Sunderland. But he knew he was losing the fight – in fact he knew of several young Scottish football players who were good enough on the field but could not cope with living away from home – so he shook hands with young Quinn and wished him well.

The grapevine told Maley this almost immediately after it happened. It was now that Maley decided to make his second bid. The afternoon of 8 December was absolutely foul, with rain cancelling both Junior and Senior games, but 15 December saw Quinn playing what turned out to be his last game for Smithston Albion. This was against Broxburn Athletic and they won 3-0, with Quinn scoring a marvellous first goal, but the chronicler of the *Kirkintilloch Gazette* tells how the home supporters, 'imbued with fresh lung power as the result of the stoppage of a passing beer bottler's cart, loudly urged on their pets [sic].'

It seems to have been quite a surreal occasion, for as Robbie Burns says in 'Tam O'Shanter'

> *The wind blews as it wad blaw its last,*
> *The rattlin showers rose on the blast,*
> *The speedy gleams the darkness swallowed,*
> *Loud, deep and lang the thunder bellowed.*

It was December and dark. The players did not even have a half-time interval, but at the end of the first half (or first 'moiety', as the *Gazette* reporter – who clearly had learned some French at school – calls it) they merely turned round on the park, the referee fearing that the game might not be able to be finished before darkness fell.

The president of the Scottish Junior Football Association was there, and given the number of 'senior club agents', the *Gazette* tells us that 'seldom has there been such a display of hats and cigars to watch the Smithston Albion'. One of the hats was worn by Willie Maley. He was very impressed with Quinn, and at the end of the match, in the shelter of the primitive pavilion, approached Quinn and offered him a trial. Quinn delighted him by agreeing – but only to a trial. Still, Maley had already got further with Quinn than the other managers had.

Maley was slightly encouraged by the feeling that this was a genuine, home-loving Croy lad, with impeccable Irish and Catholic credentials. Maley, himself a strict Catholic, abhorred sectarianism and would always be willing to give Protestants a chance to play for Celtic if they were good enough, but he knew that Irish Catholics would have a strong emotional pull to this new enterprise called the Celtic Football and Athletic Club. The fact that Quinn had turned down Sunderland meant that he would not be likely to join any other English team. Celtic, on the other hand, were successful and Irish. In only twelve years of existence, they had won the Scottish Cup three times and the Scottish League four times. Maley was at pains to stress that he was building a young team to continue and enhance the already impressive reputation of the club.

Based in Glasgow, they were also very local to Croy, being no more than twenty minutes away on the train. Celtic would seem to be the logical choice, given the proximity and Maley's willingness to play the Irish card when it suited him. Maley was convinced he was onto a winner here, but the young man would need a little persuasion…

TWO

QUINN EMERGING

Willie Maley, the genial and energetic manager of Celtic Football Club, did not often find this attitude. Here was a boy who seemed born to play for Celtic. A second-generation Irish lad, very polite and clearly of good character, was actually refusing to sign for Celtic! Maley was prepared to take his reasons at face value, for he did not think there was any other hidden, more subtle intent… he just found them strange.

Quinn's first reason was that he simply didn't think he was good enough, and his second was that he didn't want to leave his folks in Croy. Maley looked across the table at the earnest, curly headed, moustachioed young man and said gently that he (Maley) was prepared to be the judge of the first problem and that he certainly considered that Quinn was good enough, for he and his informants had now seen him several times playing for Smithston Albion.

Maley had indeed been impressed by his physique, his speed, his ability to cross a ball and his ability to take a goal. He would have played Quinn in a trial under an assumed name in a friendly for Celtic against Hibs on 29 December 1900, but for a knee injury. Now, however, Maley, fearing that someone else might get there first, was in Croy to offer him terms. Surprisingly, Quinn was not as tall as Maley had thought he was, but of course Maley had only seen him in the context of a football match where the other players had, quite frankly, seemed to suffer from malnourishment. But Maley had seen enough football to know that ability was there. Quinn would have to work hard, though. Giving up the mines would be a tremendous step in the right direction. Maley, a middle-class, second-generation Irishman and son of a soldier, had never been down a mine and had not the slightest desire of ever doing so, but he had seen what that job did to men.

The second reason, Jimmy's reluctance to leave Croy, was more psychologically complicated. Maley had been told that Quinn had previously turned down Sunderland because of fears of homesickness, but this was Glasgow! There really was no huge problem here, for there was a good rail link to Croy and, although in an ideal world Maley would have loved his players to live in lodgings within 200 yards of the new impressive Celtic Park, in practice he could not insist on this. In the case of Quinn, he could travel every day if he wished to.

It had taken Maley some time to work out the real problem. The boy was, in fact, afraid of Glasgow. He had lived in Croy all his twenty-two years, was a hero in the locality for his football exploits, had no problem attracting the attention of young women and clearly got on well with his excellent parents and siblings, whom Maley had now met. In addition, Quinn loved Smithston Albion. They would soon be engaged in cup competitions, and there was always the chance that young Quinn could win himself an International Junior cap for Scotland. Glasgow, on the other hand, was huge and potentially very frightening for a youngster from a small mining village. Maley must have been amused at the thought of such a well-built young man being afraid of the large city in which he (Maley) had himself lived almost all his life.

Maley knew that he possessed a certain charisma and could be very persuasive on occasion. This was the time to turn on the charm. He had noticed that the young man was visibly weakening in his resolve not to become a professional footballer, and he thought that this might be the chance to strike by playing the parental card. It was Sunday 30 December 1900, close enough to the New Year, and Jimmy's mother offered Maley a dram. Maley said 'Thank you very much, Mrs Quinn, but only after I can persuade this young man to sign this document…' Jimmy looked at his parents, smiled at Maley, and signed what was a provisional and temporary document, meaning that Quinn was a Celtic player for only a month. It would allow him to play in the Inter City League game against Third Lanark tomorrow afternoon, for the knee knock seemed to have cleared up.

The Inter City League was a competition that no-one really cared about. The main thing was the Scottish League, and then of course, in the New Year, the Scottish Cup. But the Inter City League did give Maley a chance to try out some of his fringe players, to nurse some back after an injury and in this case to give an opportunity to the talented youngster from Croy. Maley was convinced that he had something here.

The form signed, Maley then invited the Quinns, father and son, to come to Glasgow on the Tuesday as well, New Year's Day 1901, to watch the game against Rangers. Jimmy would almost certainly not be playing in that game – unless of course Celtic were hit by more injuries – but it would give Jimmy's father a chance to meet young Jimmy's new teammates. Then, Maley thought, the boy's homesickness would be put to an early test. Celtic, due to play Rangers again in the Scottish Cup on 12 January – a game already being hyped up by the media as the 'cup-tie of the century' – had booked a few days at the Lorne Hotel on the island of Rothesay for preparation. Would Jimmy like to come along?

That Sunday night, after Maley departed to the railway station, suitably refreshed by a couple of drams to see the old year out (and delighted that he had not been in the house of strict Scottish Presbyterians, who would certainly never have offered him a dram on a Sunday), the Quinn household was in a fervour. Jimmy was shaken by the experience and the knowledge that he was now a player of the great Glasgow Celtic. Tomorrow he was going to play for them, admittedly in a meaningless game, but then he and his father would go and see them at Ibrox playing Rangers, and Maley had agreed to meet them outside the ground. Then to Rothesay to train with mighty men like Barney Battles, Sandy McMahon and Johnnie Campbell!

Philip and Catherine, although in some ways sharing their son's apprehension about the whole business, were proud. Philip, in particular, was beginning to see and experience the drawbacks of a life down the pits with its danger to health, and the life of a professional football player seemed far better. Young Jimmy might get injured, of course, and his career might not last too long, but there would be loads of fresh air, good wholesome food, he would be fit and healthy – and of course he would earn far higher wages. If only Jimmy were not so shy outside his own environment... but that Mr Maley seemed a decent and honest gentleman.

Philip was working the following day, Monday 31 December, Hogmanay, so Jimmy went to Celtic Park on his own for what would be his debut. When he got there, he was met by Maley, who sprung a surprise. How would he like to play at centre forward that day, rather than on the left wing? Maley had decided that he would like to keep Johnnie Campbell for the Rangers game the following day, so there was a vacancy in the centre. Quinn was hardly likely to argue, so he appeared in his debut as a centre forward. His hands visibly trembled as he put on his green-and-white, vertical-striped jersey and he did not dare tell Maley that his ankle was giving him a little bother.

The crowd was about 5,000, and the game ended up a 1-1 draw. Quinn did not score Celtic's goal, but was reasonably pleased with his own performance, even though he aggravated his ankle. His teammates, like Sandy McMahon and John Divers, were helpful and supportive, and at the end Maley made a point of coming to him and shaking his hand. Maley had seen enough to further convince him that he had made a good choice here, and Quinn felt happy as he got his tram to Queen Street Station, then his train back to Croy.

It was New Year. Hogmanay saw the supper and ball of Smithston Albion in the Reading Room of Smithston. The Reading Room was the venue for most local social occasions, for Croy and Smithston were what were known as 'dry': they possessed no pub – such was the influence of the priest. On special occasions like this, however, a blind eye would be turned to the 'import' of alcohol from Kilsyth or Kirkintilloch. Chairman Mr McLay of Smithston Albion talked about their great performances in winning the Midland League and referred to their grievances about losing the Dumbartonshire Cup. 1901, he felt sure, would see the Albion making an impact on the Scottish Junior Cup. He did not mention Quinn's temporary move to Celtic. He knew about it (indeed all of Croy knew, for it was difficult to keep such news quiet) and was delighted for the youngster, but it was all as yet unofficial and he did not want to embarrass Jimmy.

What 1901 would bring for the Quinn family, nobody knew. Certainly Jimmy looked happy, thought his mother and father, when he came in after the supper and ball with that nice Annie Lang girl, but how would he cope in Glasgow with big crowds watching him? Jimmy even became nervous when Smithston Albion had a couple of hundred people watching them. Curiously, his brothers were less bothered. Celtic were reputed to attract more than 10,000 some days. Jimmy said he had a good game today in front of 5,000 and there was of course tomorrow to look forward to; Jimmy would enjoy watching his new team playing against Rangers.

What would 1901 bring to the rest of the world? The South African War was proving a difficult one to resolve. Far too many young men were being killed there, however hard the authorities tried to disguise it. To think that Jimmy was worried about going to places like Glasgow and Rothesay – it could have been South Africa! With the Conservatives back in power, that war might go on for a while.

The Quinns and the Irish in general were ambivalent about South Africa. Some hotheads in the village were quite noisily triumphant whenever the British sustained a loss there, even though other young men in the village were serving in the British Army. The Quinns knew, for example, of Private Michael Gallagher, who was in the Gordon Highlanders – a nice young man who would write back to say that he had eaten nothing but dry bread for days. England and Scotland had done some terrible things to Ireland, but as far as the Quinns were concerned it was buried in the past. The family were now Scottish and young Jimmy, if he were good enough, might even play for Scotland!

The following day's trip to Ibrox to see the game was not without its problems. Old Philip, being illiterate, could not read station names and young Jimmy was still fairly unfamiliar with Glasgow. Nevertheless, Maley had told Jimmy to make for St Enoch's and a train would take him to the home of Rangers. He had managed to get to Celtic Park the previous day, so there should be no problem for the village lad in getting himself and his father to Ibrox.

It being New Year's Day, the trains were crowded and the game itself had generated quite a great deal of excitement. Men were seen arguing vociferously about the game and drink was in plentiful supply. There was little unpleasantness, however, for everyone seemed to be full of the joys of the New Year of 1901. One or two men gave Jimmy a funny look, as if they had recognised him from the Third Lanark game of the day before, but maybe Jimmy was just being too self conscious.

When they arrived at the front gate, Maley, as promised, was there to greet them and give them a couple of free tickets. The men beside them in the stand said confidently that there would be about 30,000 folk there that day. The Quinns had never seen such a mass of people before and were totally amazed at the noise the cheering, the singing and the general atmosphere. Rangers looked as if they were to win the Scottish League and Jimmy noted that they seemed to have more supporters than Celtic did. This was to be expected, for it was their home ground, but there were one or two knots of men on the terracing supporting green rosettes and cheering when the green and white vertical stripes were doing well.

Jimmy, being an outside left, paid particular attention to Rab Findlay on Celtic's left wing, for this was the man that he would have to replace. Rab had only joined the club in August and as yet had failed to make his mark. In fact, Celtic had been without a good outside left since Johnnie Campbell played there in the early 1890s, but now Campbell was needed in the centre, according to the omniscient chap sitting beside them. Jimmy would hardly have failed to notice that Findlay was slow to the ball, and that Rangers were the better side – although Sandy McMahon scored a fine goal for Celtic late in the game.

The train trip home was less pleasant than the outward journey. A fight broke out when someone said something offensive about the Irish, and quite a few of the passengers were blatantly the worse for drink. Jimmy was glad to reach Croy, although he was comforted by the knowledge that one or two of the weasel types who did not like Celtic had looked at him, seen his bulk, and thought better of saying anything.

Back home that night, Jimmy lay in his bed and wondered. How would he cope with everyone looking at him, his name being shouted, the huge crowd – which naturally would include more than a few who would not like him or Celtic? Still, there was definitely a tingle of excitement there.

Celtic had a game against Hearts the following day. It was another of these Inter City League games, and Maley decided against playing Quinn. The boy was still slightly injured from Monday and, in any case, Maley wished to experiment with others. But it was off to Rothesay immediately afterwards so that Celtic could prepare for Rangers' visit to Parkhead.

Quinn had to meet everyone at Celtic Park. Maley did the honours, introducing him to all his teammates who had not already met him. Some eyed him with a mixture of curiosity and suspicion. Naturally any newcomer is a potential threat to someone's place in the team, but Maley was very strict that everyone was to make the new lad welcome: 'He has quality', he said.

Following the crossing to Rothesay (the first time that Quinn had seen the sea), the team walked up a hill to the Lorne Hotel, a large institution with ample fields behind for practice. There was training in the mornings, then lunch, then a practice game in the afternoon, then entertainment in the hotel. It was totally beyond Quinn's comprehension, but he found he was loving it. He was befriended by the reserve goalkeeper called Willie Donnelly, himself a comparative newcomer to the squad. Dan McArthur, the normal goalkeeper, was injured and Willie had played in the game at Ibrox on New Year's Day.

Jimmy really enjoyed the practice games in the afternoon, playing them hard and enjoying his jousts with Big Bob Davidson, a rugged defender. He was delighted to get the better of him on one or two occasions, and once crossed for McMahon to score a great header, but he noticed that Davidson had no qualms or scruples about dishing out the 'raw meat' as it was called, namely the hard tackles. 'Get used to that, Jimmy' said Bob, 'You'll get loads of it!' He noticed with a thrill of excitement that all these mighty players were now calling him 'Jimmy'.

The food was good, but Jimmy did not like the soirees, where Maley organized all the players to do their party piece for the rest of the hotel guests, be it a recitation or a song or any other piece of entertainment. Jimmy was hopeless at that and would feign excuses like needing to visit the toilet when his turn came around. Maley laughed indulgently, but on the Thursday night, the night before their departure back to Glasgow, he asked Quinn for a quiet word.

He came straight to the point. Everyone was very impressed with Jimmy Quinn in the training games. He had with him forms for his signature as a full-time professional. Wages were £3 10 shillings per week, and £2 in the summer. For that he had to train hard and give his all for Celtic Football Club. 'You've got to be prepared to die for us, Jimmy' said Maley with a straight face, before breaking into a smile. His smile intensified ten minutes later when young Jimmy Quinn shook hands with him and signed the form. Quinn was now a Celtic player.

The fact that some of the older players were able to play a trick on him and that he was able to accept it showed that he was now welcome. He was sharing a room with Sandy McMahon, Johnnie Campbell and John Divers. All four were in the 'temperance' bar of the hotel. Rounds of soft drinks were bought, but when it came to Jimmy's turn to buy, they all said 'No! No! Keep yer hand in yer pooch, Jimmy'. An hour or so later, when they had all retired to bed, McMahon pretended to fall sound asleep, but very soon began to talk in his 'sleep', saying a few scandalous things about Maley and one of the hotel chambermaids, some Rangers players who had fouled him, then 'See that young Quinn? Widnae buy a drink! Miserable young…' Quinn was upset by this, and the next night tried all the harder to buy his round, insisting vehemently, until the other three burst out laughing! It did, however, mean that Jimmy was now one of the boys.

Celtic returned from Rothesay to Celtic Park to play Rangers in the first round of the Scottish Cup. Celtic were, of course, the holders, and Quinn knew that this trophy was very important for Celtic, as it was considered to be the Blue Riband of Scottish Football. Rangers had now won the Scottish League, which usually finished at the turn of the year in the early years of the twentieth century. Luck had decreed that the two biggest teams in Glasgow were drawn together in the Scottish Cup, and another huge crowd was expected.

Jimmy might have hoped that Rab Findlay had picked up an injury, but he hadn't. Thus Jimmy was given a pass to the Grant Stand to watch the game, along with the other reserves. This was the first time that Quinn had been to Celtic Park as a Celtic player to see a really big match. The crowd was yet again 30,000. It was a magnificent stadium, the home of Scotland for international games against England, and the pride of the Glasgow Irish community. The crowd was about the same as had been at Ibrox for the New Year game, but this time the score was different. Celtic won 1-0, although it was an own goal. Jimmy had to admit that Rab Findlay had a good game on the left wing, and in any case he was delighted for his team. Goalkeeper Dan McArthur was carried off, and Jimmy was sorry for him because he had only recently returned from injury – Jimmy had already developed a fondness for the dapper Dan.

Quinn's return to Croy that night was his first as a full-time Celtic footballer. Even his 'close season' wages of £2 were a lot more than he could have earned in the Gartshore Pit, and his parents were understandably very proud of their son. His days as a miner were now past him (at least temporarily), but he had to be very careful to work at his football. This meant having to be careful with what he ate, and even more so with what he drank. He mustn't get fat, he mustn't get drunk, he mustn't get ill and he must train hard, even on Sundays when he wasn't required at the ground.

The following Saturday, 19 January 1901, saw Quinn playing for the first team, and this time he was fully fit and in what he considered his proper position. It was the last game of the Scottish League – a meaningless fixture now that the League had been lost. The trip to St Mirren's new Love Street stadium was therefore more of a friendly than anything else, with Maley giving Quinn and young John Gray a try. Quinn had been told by Maley early in the week that he would get a game, and he was mentally prepared for it.

He was less prepared for the violence. The game may have been 'dead' as far as the Scottish League was concerned, but St Mirren, like most provincial teams, felt that they had a point to prove with the mighty Glasgow Celtic. Some of the tackles on Quinn seemed deliberately made in order to intimidate the youngster. But Jimmy was no stranger to the rough stuff (he had played against Harthill and other tough teams in the Juniors, after all), and refused to be either rattled or provoked into retaliation.

Celtic had started off with the wind and Quinn's pace was instrumental in the fine early showing of the forward line, which took full advantage of the conditions in their favour. He had the good fortune to score a goal himself inside the first quarter of an hour, when a ball rebounded off a defender and he was on the spot to bang the ball home. He then passed for Campbell to score the third goal after Hodge had scored the second. Quinn must have felt himself in heaven as the referee brought the first half to a halt with Celtic leading 4-1.

Maley, however, was stern in his warnings. 'They have now got the wind… watch out for the rough stuff… don't involve yourselves…it's going to be tough' were among the things he said. His warnings were justified. St Mirren began the second half the way that Celtic had begun the first, and before ten minutes had gone, they had pulled the score back to 4-3. Poor Willie Donnelly in Celtic's goal was badly at fault with the second and then the third one rebounded wickedly off a post.

What Quinn was now noticing was his sheer lack of pace and stamina. He had spent himself in the first half and had little left. To an extent, this was due to his lack of full-time training, but it was also due to his inability to pace himself. It was one thing with the wind behind you and the team on top of the game, but it was another when the contest was going against the team, and Quinn had been forced back to help out the hard-pressed defence.

For a spell, however, Celtic took a grip of the game and, after one or two desperate clearances, Quinn was signalled at by Maley from the touchline to move up the field and hope for a breakaway. The game continued its tough course in the intensifying wind and rain when suddenly Sandy McMahon and a St Mirren player were involved in a scuffle. Players from both sides were helping the referee to restore order when Quinn was aware of a push in the back and 'Catholic bastard' being shouted at him. Some idiots had jumped the rope and invaded the park!

Fortunately there were not many of them, and the Paisley constables were soon able to get hold of them, but Quinn noticed that Maley and Celtic's president, John Glass, had been involved in a scuffle as well. In spite of the potential seriousness of this situation, Quinn had to smile to himself. Neither Maley nor Glass were exactly lightweights, and here were one or two piteously undernourished youths (who looked as if they could do with a good bowl of soup) having a go at them!

It was all a learning experience. Jimmy congratulated himself on not getting himself involved in the fracas, although he was a little taken aback by it. Such things happened in Junior football, but he honestly thought that they did not happen at the Senior level. The game restarted, but the referee, as if fearing further trouble, seemed to shorten the game by a few minutes. Celtic thus held out to win 4-3. The exhausted Quinn had to drag himself off the field at the end, but how he enjoyed the luxury of the hot bath provided at the Love Street ground!

This game would be the end of an era, for three days later, Queen Victoria died, having been on the throne for a world record sixty-four years. Maley, being a royalist, insisted that the players came in for training with a black tie on. Quinn, of course, complied with Maley's instruction, but could not help thinking that it was all very unnecessary. Glasgow more or less closed down for the day of her funeral, Saturday 2 February – and there would be no football that day.

The League season now being over, all that remained for Celtic in 1901 was the cup competitions, particularly the Scottish Cup, and various friendlies. Quinn was, of course, relegated to the reserves or the junior teams. He could hardly complain about this. Rab Findlay was playing well enough and Quinn realised that it would be some time before he could up a gear and cope with the sheer pace of the first team.

By the end of February, however, Maley clearly thought that Quinn was worth another run. In a friendly against a Hearts XI at Tynecastle in the moribund Inter City League, on a day when several men were on international duty, it was reported that 'Quinn… is here to stay' and the scribes were impressed by his ability to take punishment and keep going. He scored a goal when the Hearts goalkeeper dropped the ball and 'Quinn, dashing in, scored to the chagrin of the home supporters'. In a game against Queen's Park at the beginning of March, he was favourably compared to Johnnie Campbell, playing 'splendidly on the left'.

Then Quinn got his biggest break. Rab Findlay's weak knee started to play up – he would suffer from chronic cartilage problems throughout his career – and Maley called Jimmy in to his office one day to tell him that he was in the team for the Scottish Cup semi-final against St Mirren at Parkhead on 23 March. Neutral venues were only used for the final in 1901, and thus it was that Quinn made his Scottish Cup debut at Parkhead that day. Remembering his previous experience against St Mirren earlier that year, he was somewhat apprehensive.

It was bright but windy, and 17,000 came to Celtic Park to see the green-and-whites take on St Mirren. Jimmy's father was there, as indeed were several of his friends from Croy, where there was now talk of forming a 'brake club' or charabanc group to go to every game in Glasgow or the immediate environs. The crowd saw a great match in which Quinn played well and Celtic emerged victorious 1-0. Campbell scored the only goal of the contest, but St Mirren had proved that they were 'no slouches', as the *Glasgow Herald* put it.

Celtic were into the Scottish Cup final. They had won the trophy in 1899 and 1900, and this was their opportunity to win the trophy for the third year in a row. Their opponents were Hearts, the Edinburgh team who had won the Scottish Cup in 1896 and the League in 1897, and who possessed at least two tremendous players in defender Charlie Thomson and the impressive inside forward Bobby Walker. Quinn found himself hoping that Findlay's knee would not improve, but he also felt that, even if it did, he himself had played well enough in the St Mirren semi-final to justify inclusion in the final. In the event, although Findlay's knee was showing signs of amelioration, it had not yet made sufficient progress for him to be risked, and Maley was able to tell Quinn that the left wing spot would be his.

The team were taken away to Rothesay again for a break immediately before the big match, scheduled for 6 April 1901. Quinn could not help noticing this time that even the experienced men like Battles and Campbell (who had played in last week's Scotland *v*. England game at Crystal Palace along with Bobby Walker of Hearts) were on edge. Maley himself, however much he pretended insouciance, was also tense, and the team talks and get-togethers were laced with a certain uneasiness. Queen's Park and Vale of Leven had won the Cup three years in succession, but that was in the early days of the 1870s. Celtic would be the first side to do so in the modern, professional era. The Scottish Cup was a very important competition.

Quinn shared a room with Willie Loney, the centre half who had enjoyed a good first season. Willie came from Denny, not too far from Croy, and they became friends. Willie was, like Jimmy, shy at first and sometimes gave the impression of being overawed by the worldly-wise characters of the team. It was only natural that the two should drift towards each other. In later years, it would not be unknown for the pair of them to enjoy a pint of beer in each other's company – when Maley wasn't around!

The Scottish Cup final was to be played at Ibrox. There had been a great deal of rain for a couple of days previously, and as a result the pitch was wet and slippery. This was not a great concern for Quinn, who often felt that he revelled in such conditions, but the surface would sadly be Celtic's downfall in this game.

High admission charges may well have deterred a few, but it was still a disappointing turnout of 15,000, which included a sizeable contingent from the East. Indeed, the scribe in *The Scotsman* (whose account of the game is manifestly pro-Hearts) says that the 'sympathies of the majority of the crowd were behind Hearts'. The crowd saw one of the best Cup Finals of them all, albeit with a tragic outcome for Celtic and Quinn. It was Dan McArthur in Celtic's goal who had a shocker. The first goal went in when the ball spun wickedly off the ground and through McArthur's hands. Although Willie McOustra equalized through a header from a free-kick, McArthur again was at fault when he punched a ball that he should have clutched. The ball broke to Bell of Hearts, he shot and it went in after taking a deflection.

After half-time, Hearts, with the wind now behind them, scored again. It was a fine piece of work involving Thomson and Walker (and another McArthur fumble), and Maley put it rather well when he described Celtic's prospects with the score at 1-3 against them as the 'reverse of bright'. But this Celtic team was not without character, and it was at this point that Quinn, who had hitherto been anonymous on the left wing with the ball seldom coming near him, came into his own. Celtic started to feed him and the right winger, Willie McOustra, and the pair of them began to charge down the wings, Quinn in particular using his strength to barge a way through.

Celtic pulled one back after seventy-one minutes when Quinn beat about six or seven Hearts men to score a great goal (although some sources say that McOustra got a touch on the ball, the goal is generally accredited to Quinn), and then well within the last ten minutes, Quinn forced a corner, took it himself and Sandy McMahon rose like a bird to head home and put Celtic level.

It should have stayed like that and a replay would have been on the cards. Indeed Celtic, with Quinn now outstanding, might even have scored a winner, but the winning goal came desperately late – and at the other end. Once again Dan McArthur, whose career had hitherto been exemplary and deserving of more than the three meagre international caps that he earned, failed to hold a harmless-looking long drive and in the scrimmage a Hearts player (some say Thomson, others Bell, others Houston) was on hand to smash home the loose ball.

It was a colossal disappointment for Quinn, who nevertheless was very keen to comfort the distraught McArthur. Tears flowed from more than one of his teammates, because a defeat in a Cup Final is something that is very hard to take, and it meant that Celtic only had the Glasgow Charity Cup to compete for this year if they were to avoid their first barren season since 1897. A few friendly matches were now played, with Quinn given a run in various positions in the forward line.

The Charity Cup was played in May at the Exhibition Grounds, Gilmorehill. The convention was that the games were played at the end of the season and that the players were not paid for their services – what they would have earned going to charity. The semi-final against Rangers on 2 May was a draw in beautiful weather, then the replay the following night saw Quinn at his best as he helped John Hodge to score the only goal of the game. Sadly, Quinn missed the drawn final against Third Lanark (when he had a leg injury) on 9 May. The replay had to be delayed until 23 May (which was Victoria Day – quite poignant this year as she had died in January), for Celtic were on tour in the Highlands. In one of these tour games, injuries to other players compelled Quinn to play a match against the Northern Counties at right-back!

The Charity Cup final replay was again played at Gilmorehill. The side performed very badly and lost 3-0. Quinn, however, had a 'capital game on the left' and managed 'a splendid effort which deserved better reward' before Thirds had opened the scoring. It was, however, another horror for Dan McArthur, and Celtic finished 1901 with nothing.

Yet Quinn had made his mark in his first season. The fans, although naturally disappointed at the team's performances, were nevertheless able to say that there were a few signs that something good was happening, and young Quinn was clearly part of it. It was clear that the team were in transition. They had had some brilliant seasons in the 1890s, but perhaps it was now time for the old guard to be cleared out. Rangers had taken over as League Champions for the last three seasons; Celtic's team was still developing. Maley would write articles in the football papers, pointing to youngsters like Loney and Quinn, telling the supporters that that was where lay the future of Celtic. Patience, however, would be required.

As is always the case with youth policies, the supporters would need a little convincing. Maley was concerned that Celtic might see their fans drifting away. He realised that Celtic, with their hinterland of the Irish in Glasgow's East End, should have more fans than other teams, but he had been a little alarmed when he saw that the gates and receipts in 1901 had been less than they had been in the early years. Yet he would not be panicked. It would take time to build a good team, and youngsters like Quinn were only the beginning.

Quinn was now the automatic first-team choice for the left wing position. He received consistently good newspaper reports, with phrases like 'Quinn showing pace' and 'Quinn barging through' appearing frequently. More tellingly, there was often a lack of criticism. Reporters of this era could be quite cruel on a player with damning comments such as 'poor distribution marred his efforts' or, even more brutally, 'poor and will never improve'. Noticeably, Quinn, unlike some others in the team, tended to avoid this sort of adverse report.

What he would have noticed, however, was that he was frequently the source of an attack by an opponent. Referees were more lenient a hundred years ago than they are now, and a talented player like Quinn would be singled out for rough treatment – especially in the early years of his career. For example, the holiday weekend of September 1901 saw Jimmy fouled mercilessly on the Saturday by St Mirren's Jackson in front of a rabid Paisley crowd, then on the Monday in the final of the Glasgow Exhibition Trophy at Gilmorehill by Rangers' brutal right-back Nick Smith. He would, of course, cross swords with Smith in the future.

Mercifully, Jimmy did not retaliate to all this (although in later years he would not always be so docile) and although his legs were obviously black and blue, he managed to persuade Maley that he was able to play in the following Saturday's Glasgow Cup game against Clyde. This was an easier encounter, won comfortably by Celtic, but it was one game too far for Quinn. He picked up a slight knock (not in itself serious), which aggravated his pre-existing injuries and was seen to limp off at the end. This caused him to miss a few games.

When he returned on 28 September 1901 it was to play at centre forward as Maley tried Findlay on the left wing once again. Although Celtic won this game at Kilmarnock, the move was not deemed a success and the important game against Rangers at Ibrox saw Campbell back at centre forward and Quinn at outside left.

It was probably this game at Ibrox in the Scottish League that made everyone sit up and take notice of Jimmy Quinn. In the first place he impressed everyone by his courageous running at Nick Smith, knowing that he was likely to get some more ill treatment – indeed, at one point Smith received a 'finger wagging' from the referee – and Quinn's crossing of a ball was very impressive. Celtic were 2-1 down late in the game. It was beginning to look as if some of the forwards, particularly the veterans Campbell and McMahon, were on the point of giving up, when, with only a few minutes remaining, Quinn picked up a ball on his left wing halfway inside the Rangers half.

The Rangers defence fell back and his colleagues screamed for a pass, but Jimmy recognised the space he was being afforded for what it was – respect for his ability and fear for what he could do. 'Not unlike a bull in a Spanish arena', Jimmy lowered his head and charged in a diagonal direction towards the goal. He was tackled once or twice but persevered and got through the defence to equalize. The goal was greeted with acclaim by the Celtic fans, and Maley was ecstatic. Indeed, Quinn might have scored again and won the game, but the goalkeeper denied him.

The team was now playing better than it had for some time, and progress was made to the Glasgow Cup final to play Rangers – for the third time that season before the end of October! The final itself was interesting, with Quinn playing well and Celtic fighting back to earn a draw, but the real fun began after the game. The Glasgow FA, who had decided that Ibrox was to be the venue for the game irrespective of who was playing, also decreed that Ibrox would be the venue for the replay. Celtic, not unnaturally, objected, demanding that the game be played at Parkhead, or even a neutral venue like Cathkin or Gilmorehill (Hampden had not yet been built), but the Glasgow FA dug their heels in. Celtic refused to play, and on 17 December 1901 the Glasgow Cup was awarded to Rangers. Thus was Jimmy Quinn deprived of a chance of his first medal.

Despite this setback, League form at the start of the season was good. Quinn was given another go in the centre forward position against Queen's Park on 19 October. He scored the only goal 'at the call of time' from that position, even though *The Scotsman* says that 'Quinn was a poor substitute for Campbell in the centre and several chances went begging'. Quinn then missed a couple of games through injury in November, but played in a fine win at the new Dens Park, Dundee.

It was a very competitive League that season, and both Celtic and Rangers dropped points – in Celtic's case to Hearts and Queen's Park. The penultimate game of the campaign was on Saturday 28 December 1901 against Kilmarnock at Celtic Park in 'wretched conditions' with a wet pitch, a crowd of only 3,000 (for many had thought the game would be off) and darkness setting in so early that the referee considered abandoning the game. The kick-off was 2 p.m. but even so, darkness fell soon after 3 p.m. and 'the movements of the players could be followed only with difficulty'. In spite of all this, Celtic won 4-2, with Quinn outstanding. In particular his 'clever pass' for Hodge's goal was singled out for praise.

All this meant that if Celtic could beat Rangers on New Year's Day at Parkhead, they would win the League. Only two things prevented Celtic from becoming Champions. One was that Quinn was injured again, having strained a muscle while doing the splits on the wet pitch against Kilmarnock, and the other was an eccentric performance by the referee Mr Nesbit of Cowdenbeath – who may have celebrated the Scottish New Year a little too enthusiastically the night before. McMahon tripped him up and was sent off, and several others on both sides should have shared the same punishment. The game disintegrated into a shambles as Rangers won 4-2.

Quinn, watching this game from the Grant Stand with his father and brother, must have been upset at missing a League medal in those circumstances. Yet he had a great deal to be happy about. He had now been with Celtic for a year, and in that time he had made great strides. The left wing spot was now his own, and he had clearly earned a place in Maley's affections – which several others manifestly had not. Two things concerned him, however. One was his susceptibility to injuries and the other was Celtic's inability to win anything. The former would be a problem all his career; the latter would be solved, but only in time.

The loss of the Scottish League on the first day of 1902 was a harbinger of things to come. 1902 would be a bittersweet year for Celtic, with the team playing very well but not always having the luck or the break of the ball that was required, except on one famous occasion. It would be the one that would live long in the memory of the Celtic crowds as the morning star of the great things to come.

Quinn was comparatively free from injuries in the spring of 1902 as Celtic mounted yet another assault on the Scottish Cup. The unlikely venue of Arbroath on Burns Day of 25 January was a potential banana skin for the Celtic team, who only five years previously had appalled their supporters by going down to Arthurlie. Gayfield has the deserved reputation of being the coldest ground in Scotland when the wind is coming from the east, as it was that day. Intermittent snow showers made conditions worse, although the statement in the local press that the 'snow fell in pancakes' is a picturesque exaggeration of the truth, one feels.

The Angus men were far from overawed by their mighty opponents and right-back Carrie knew how to tackle Quinn, who seemed at first to be put off by the proximity of the crowd and the terrible conditions. At one point Arbroath were 2-1 up, but Willie Orr equalized with a long-range drive and then Quinn for once shook off the shackles of Carrie to pass to Sandy McMahon, who scored the winner.

The month of February then saw a prolonged struggle to get the better of Hearts. In fact they played four games in that calendar month – all against the men from Tynecastle. The first was on 1 February and it was a glorified friendly in the so-called Inter City League. Quinn was rested that day in favour of a young debutant called Davie Hamilton, who would in time become a great colleague of Jimmy. Tynecastle was frozen on 8 February for the Scottish Cup game, but Celtic had arrived by the time any decision could be taken. The game then went ahead, but as a friendly – a decision that does not seem to have been made on the basis of consideration for players' welfare! The real tie was staged the following week on 15 February in front of 23,000 fans and Quinn delighted the Celtic contingent in the fourth minute when he scored with a 'low slanting shot'. Hearts, however, came back, scored through

Charlie Thomson and (according to the manifestly biased writer of *The Scotsman*) 'were unlucky not to add to their tally'.

Thus on 22 February, for the third week in succession, Quinn lined up against Hearts, whose full-back, Jimmy Hogg, he was now on first-name terms with. Twenty-five thousand were there at Parkhead, but Celtic this time had two advantages. They had just come back from Rothesay where they had been training – something that clearly helped them to bind together – and Hearts were without their star inside man Bobby Walker, whose father had died recently.

Yet it was Hearts who scored first, before most of the crowd had got through the primitive Parkhead payboxes. Celtic settled after this and, realising that Quinn was on song, supplied him with loads of ammunition. Before half-time he had fed his left wing partner Sandy McMahon to equalize; halfway through the second half, he did the same for McMahon to win the game. The wonder was that Celtic did not score more goals.

After sundry friendlies, in which Quinn continued to distinguish himself, the semi-final brought Celtic to Love Street, Paisley – the scene of Quinn's competitive debut more than a year previously. By now, Celtic against St Mirren games were a byword for tough, competitive play. Once again it was a fierce encounter, but Celtic edged through 3-2, and once again Quinn attracted favourable Press comments.

Quinn was lucky in that he belonged to a great Celtic team, which by 1902 was probably better than Rangers. Rangers had won all their outstanding Scottish League games and were champions for the fourth time in a row, but most football people considered that Celtic were rapidly becoming the better side and well worthy of their fourth consecutive Scottish Cup final appearance. Hibs were the other finalists, so it was the first ever 'all green' or 'all Irish' Cup Final.

But before that happened two events occurred, one concerning Quinn personally and the other concerning football, which would throw a great shadow over the calendar year of 1902. The first was on 20 March when Annie Lang, a domestic servant of Drummylass Cottages, Cumbernauld, gave birth to a daughter whom she called Sarah. There was not much doubt who the father was, and indeed the birth certificate has Jimmy's signature on it – acknowledging his paternity.

Illegitimacy in Scotland during the early years of the twentieth century, particularly in the mining communities, was hardly unusual, but a minor mystery arises as to why Jimmy did not marry Annie immediately. He did marry her on 31 December 1902, some nine months later, and every indication was that it was a long and happy marriage until Jimmy's death in 1945. But why was Jimmy not shamed into 'doing the decent thing' at the time?

The answer may be in that the Lang family were non-Catholic. In 1902, in Croy, this would have been a major stumbling block, and it may be that Jimmy (with the backing of his family and priest) refused to marry her – or indeed was told not to marry her until such time as she 'converted'. It may be that Jimmy, with so much else going on in his life, was not sure of his feelings for Annie and did not want to be bulldozed into a marriage so suddenly.

It is even possible that the priest and his parents, far from not allowing Jimmy to marry Annie, tried to insist that he did marry her and that Jimmy refused, until Mr Maley was called in. Maley was never one for any kind of scandal with his players, and his intervention may have swung the balance. Perhaps Maley arrived in Croy one night in the latter part of 1902 to read Jimmy the riot act, compelling him to make an honest woman of Annie and to legitimise Sarah.

Whatever the case may be, the wedding duly took place on Hogmanay 1902 at Croy Chapel House, Cumbernauld 'After Banns according to the Roman Catholic Church', from which we may assume that Annie had now accepted Jimmy's faith. Jimmy and Annie did not have much of a honeymoon – on the day after their marriage, Jimmy played in a 3-3 draw at Ibrox on New Year's Day 1903!

The marriage seems to have been a happy one, lasting until Jimmy's death in 1945. Annie survived until 1955. After Sarah, there were another nine children born – Philip in 1904, Catherine in 1905, Annie in 1908, James in 1910, Mary in 1912, Margaret in 1913, John ('Jock') in 1916 (this young man was later to die in the Second World War), Anthony (who was the father of Jimmy Quinn the Younger who played in the late 1960s for Celtic) in 1918, and Elizabeth in 1921. They lived in various houses – Smithston Row, Barbegs, Coronation Row and, latterly, 45 Cuilmuir Terrace – but they never moved away from Croy. On the birth certificates of his children, Jimmy describes himself as a coal miner until young James is born in 1910, when Jimmy senior is a football player, but reverts to being a coal miner by 1918.

The major football event in Scotland was a tragedy, which took place at Ibrox on 5 April. At the Scotland *v*. England international, a wooden stand collapsed and twenty-six people were killed, with scores more being injured. It would have been very tempting for Celtic people to state that it would not have happened if Celtic Park had been chosen for the international (as it had been hitherto) but the matter was far too sad for that.

Quinn, who was brought up with the possibility of loss of life in pits and was regularly appalled by the needless casualties in the ongoing war in South Africa, was horrified and upset. Indeed, so was all of Scottish society, but the practical point about it was that the Scottish Cup final of 1902, due to be played at Ibrox on 12 April, now had to be played at Celtic Park on 26 April. In fact, it became a home game for Celtic because Hampden Park was not yet built and there was no other ground big enough for the expected large crowd.

Quinn's second Scottish Cup final was just as disappointing as the previous one, for Hibs won 1-0 in a 'dull and spiritless' game. It might have been different if Maley had grasped the nettle and played Quinn in the centre, as he was to do with such conspicuous and significant success two years later. Johnnie Campbell, the centre forward, was injured. Maley could indeed have played Jimmy through the middle and given the promising Davie Hamilton a run on the left wing, but opted instead to put the veteran McMahon in the centre with the right-footed Livingstone at inside left, leaving a space on the right wing for the comparatively untried Billy McCafferty.

This ploy did not work. The first half was listless, apart from the moment when, following a fine Quinn-Livingstone combination, the ball hit the post and rebounded to the luckless Billy McCafferty – who missed an open goal. Ex-Celt John Divers, who was now with the Edinburgh greens, repeatedly fouled Sandy McMahon as he tried to jump for Quinn's corners and neither team really got going.

The second half was little better. Hibs scored in the sixty-seventh minute with a strange goal: following a goalmouth scrimmage, McGeachan backheeled a ball through the Celtic goalkeeper's legs. Celtic redoubled their attempts, with Quinn and Livingstone outstanding, and the writer of *The Scotsman* concedes that 'the efforts put forth by the home side were worthy of a better fate', but the game finished with no further scoring.

Quinn was devastated. To lose a Scottish Cup final was as gut-wrenching in 1902 as it would be in 2002 or any other year; the pain involved in losing two Cup Finals in a row is difficult to imagine. His mood would not have been helped by the gloating triumphalism of the Hibernian players – who seemed to have a problem with Celtic, whom they blamed for impoverishing and bankrupting their team in the early 1890s. Bobby Atherton, for example, burst into a parody of a Boer War song when he sung 'Goodbye Celtic, we must leave you' and the team returned to a triumphant reception in Edinburgh, which *The Scotsman* blames for disrupting traffic and 'frightening more than a few horses'. One hopes that the Edinburgh men enjoyed their celebrations that night. More than a hundred years later, they have had no cause to do the same as far as the Scottish Cup is concerned.

Hibs would in 1902 be able to build on their triumph in the Glasgow Charity Cup on 31 May. (In 1902, teams from outside Glasgow were invited to take part to swell the coffers of the Ibrox Disaster Fund.) On a day of dreadful wind and rain, Hibs came to Hampden to beat Celtic 6-2. Quinn was played at inside right (as he had been more successfully in the semi-final against Third Lanark), and although he scored a consolation goal, he was like a fish out of water against a rampant Hibernian midfield.

But the season was not yet over, even at that late date of 31 May. Rangers had put up the Glasgow Exhibition Cup, which they won in 1901 to raise funds for the Ibrox Disaster Fund. They invited Celtic, Sunderland (the English champions) and Everton (the English runners-up) to take part. Celtic opened the tournament on 30 April by running amok over Sunderland at Celtic Park and beating them 5-1. It was only four days after the disastrous Scottish Cup final, and the miserable crowd of 4,000 perhaps indicates a certain amount of disillusion. Those who did turn up, however, saw Jimmy Quinn as his best, having a part in all the goals. Campbell had by this time returned from injury and it was a more conventional Celtic forward line.

Sunderland were taken aback by this display of power. Goalkeeper Ned Doig, a Scotland international, would say that Celtic's forwards were the best he had seen. No doubt the Sunderland man who had tried to sign Jimmy in late 1900 cursed his luck. But it was the final of this tournament that showed the world Jimmy Quinn at his best. Once again injuries were a problem for Celtic, but this time Maley did put Quinn in the centre and played Davie Hamilton on the left wing for the final against Rangers at Old Hampden Park (otherwise known as Cathkin) on the balmy evening of 17 June 1902.

Quinn displayed limitless energy and pace and, by halfway through the first half, he had scored twice. Careless defending allowed Rangers back into the game, however, and extra time was required. Two minutes remained when Celtic won a corner. Alec Crawford swung over a high one, and Jimmy Quinn rose above them all to head home a classic winner, thereby establishing his credentials for the centre forward position, winning his first medal and beginning Celtic's tradition of winning one-off trophies. The winning goal was scored in a distinctly unconventional (although legal) way. Inside forward Tommy McDermott was standing facing the goal, about to jump for the incoming delivery, when he heard the stentorian Quinn cry of 'Stey whaur ye are Tommy!' He obeyed and Jimmy hoisted himself on Tommy's back to do the needful!

The Celtic fans, who had had precious little to shout about for the last two years, had a new hero:

> Some say the Rangers are guid at fitba',
> That Smith and Gibson and Speedie are braw,
> But Jimmy Quinn, he diddled them aw',
> At the Glasgow Exhibition Oh!

The summer of 1902 was a glorious one. The South African War had ended, and there was a steady trickle of soldiers back from the war, some sadly having lost a limb in the process. On the sporting front, the cricket between England and Australia held the attention of most people, even Scotsmen, but the main event was the Coronation of King Edward VII. The event had had to be postponed because Edward needed an operation for appendicitis (one of the first ever and a very dangerous undertaking in 1902), but it eventually took place on Saturday 9 August. It was in honour of this event that 'Coronation Row' in Croy was named.

It probably was a big event in Quinn's life in that everyone was on holiday and it would be difficult not to be involved. Celtic and their fans have often been labelled as anti-Royalists, but in 1902, there would have been every reason to be carried away with the general euphoria. Even those who wished Home Rule for Ireland were convinced that it could be done under the auspices of the British Crown. Maley himself was very pro-Royalty, a curious contradiction since the monarchy would not tolerate anyone of the Roman Catholic persuasion to be married into them.

It is curious, incidentally, that of the four Coronations that took place in the twentieth century (1902, 1911, 1937 and 1953), in two of those years Celtic won an all-British Trophy, in another case it was the next year, and in the other Celtic had just won six League Championships in a row and won the Scottish Cup during that year. Perhaps Celtic and the British Royal Family do blend well together.

The fans celebrated the Coronation, but the talk would undeniably have been about the prospects for the new season, with that great youngster Quinn – whose running, shooting and physical presence marked him out as something special. The Ibrox disaster had still not gone away, for Rangers (as well as the Exhibition Trophy – which, incidentally, they expected Celtic to hand back) also organized a Club Benefit Trophy to raise additional funds after Ibrox was re-opened. The first game was Rangers v. Celtic on 20 August and yet again Jimmy Quinn scored a hat-trick in a goal feast that Celtic won 7-2. Celtic would then go on and win the tournament by beating Partick Thistle and Morton.

Yet the League campaign of 1902/03 was not a success. Too many draws and a few bad defeats meant that the Championship was lost before Christmas, albeit this time the winners were not the shell-shocked Rangers, but Hibs – who played consistently well and proved their worth the day after New Year by winning 4-0 at Parkhead. Quinn was not playing in that match, having been injured in the draw against Rangers the previous day, but he had not enjoyed a good League campaign. This may well have been because he suffered from being moved about the forward line. Davie Hamilton was too good to be stuck out on the left wing, as indeed was Johnnie Campbell in the centre, so Quinn often found himself on the right wing when both these players were available.

He also endured a phenomenon that is called 'second season syndrome' in English County Cricket. This was, of course, Quinn's third season, and although he had been very impressive in both campaigns so far, defenders were now beginning to suss him out. This often involved brutal tactics, and there was no lack of defenders in the Scottish game who knew how to do just that. He was also worth having two defenders on him, for everyone knew how dangerous he could be.

A case in point was the Glasgow Cup final of October 1902. Celtic had done well to reach the final to play Third Lanark at Ibrox. But the 'Sodgers' (as Third Lanark were called, because their full name was the 3rd Lanark Rifle Volunteers) were a fine team. Indeed, they would win the Scottish League in 1904 and the Scottish Cup in 1905. On this occasion, a few hefty challenges on Quinn in the first few minutes left him limping and virtually useless. Not for the first time, nor the last, was heard the cry 'No Quinn, no Celtic', for the rest of the team then collapsed as Third Lanark won easily.

After the New Year of 1903, a total of six attempts were made in the Scottish Cup before Celtic eventually emerged victorious over St Mirren. There were two postponements, one abandonment and two draws before eventually, on 14 February (the process having begun on 10 January), Celtic made everyone wonder what all the fuss had been about by winning 4-0 with Quinn, back on the left wing, rampaging past his defender in the heavy conditions to send over crosses galore. But after a defeat of Port Glasgow, it all came to grief for Celtic as they unaccountably collapsed 0-3 to Rangers at Ibrox.

This was the end of an era for Celtic. Maley had now decided that Campbell and McMahon (fine players both) had now done all they could for the club. They would hardly play for Celtic again and soon moved on – McMahon to Partick Thistle and Campbell to Third Lanark – leaving the forward line needing fresh blood. This would be forthcoming in men like Bennett, Somers and McMenemy. Maley, however, remained convinced that Quinn would be the coming star, even though some of the supporters were making their feelings known (in a noisy way) that they were becoming unhappy with the 'Croy boy'.

A certain amount of consolation for an otherwise depressing season was gained in the summer, when the team won the Glasgow Charity Cup. It was not only the winning of the competition but the manner of it that cheered the faithful, for Hibs were thrashed 5-0 and St Mirren 5-2. Quinn had never played well against Hibs hitherto, but on 21 May, buoyed up perhaps by the news that Annie was expecting a baby in early 1904, he rammed home a hat-trick. His second goal was a tremendous one-man show in which he 'beat everyone' as the *Glasgow Herald* hyperbolically put it and ran so fast that he was given the nickname 'The Croy Express' for the first time.

The final against St Mirren at Cathkin saw another fine Quinn performance as he scored once and fed Bennett and Loney for others. It was his first medal in this competition, but the thing that really cheered up Jimmy was the appearance at centre half of a new signing called James

Young. He, like Quinn himself, was a reluctant Celt at first and had not been a great success with Bristol Rovers, but played absolutely brilliantly in the rear in both these games. Quinn took an instant liking to the fair-haired youth with the broad Ayrshire accent, who would soon be known as 'Sunny Jim'. Quinn felt that although 1903 had been a disappointment, 1904 might well be better. Maley shared that view.

THREE

QUINN BREAKS THROUGH

Maley was thoughtful as he watched his young side go through their pre-season training at Seamill Hydro in early August 1903. Seamill Hydro had now replaced Rothesay as the 'home from home' when he needed to work with his players. Being a Hydro hotel, there was no alcohol, but there were other advantages as well, in that the players could relax and play games like table tennis and billiards. It was also very peaceful and quiet – and indeed very beautiful.

Maley was very aware that this was a new Celtic, and that it was *his* team. He would stand or fall by how well the young side did. The old guard of Bell, McMahon and Campbell (whose glory days were long behind them) were gone. They had been replaced by Young, Bennett, McMenemy and others. Symbolic of the new age would be a change in the styling of the kit. The team would now wear green and white horizontal stripes on their jersey, rather than vertical, but there would still be the all-green jersey as a change strip.

The sight of the bulky figure of Quinn made him stop and think. Not all the directors (nor indeed the supporters) shared his high opinion of the muscular lad from Croy. Quinn did have his good moments, and would always have a cherished place in the hearts of the supporters for his hat-trick in the Exhibition Trophy of 1902, but sometimes he would waste all his energy in the first half and have little left for the second. There was the feeling too that he had gone as far as he was likely to go. He was injury prone – which was perhaps a compliment to Quinn, for the opposition would identify him as the danger man – and, in addition, neither Maley nor Quinn himself could make up his mind where his best position was. He was a fine left winger, Maley thought, but his best position was possibly in the middle of the field.

There were other factors in the equation: it all depended on other players that were available. Davie Hamilton was a fine left winger and really could not be denied his place forever, and Alec Bennett looked as if he could be a good centre forward as well as a right winger. One thing that Maley was sure about, however, was that the lion-hearted Quinn would try his best wherever he was put. Maley liked that in his players – a man who would play for the club, a man who considered the success of the team to be more important than any personal glory. In this sense, Quinn was an unpretentious, unambitious sort of fellow. There would be no tantrums if he did not get his own way.

What was really required for the fans was the capture of a major Scottish trophy, either the Scottish Cup or the League. No-one really bothered about the Inter City League, which was now being squeezed out even more by the expansion of the Scottish League. The Glasgow Cup was fine, but limited to Glasgow teams, and the Glasgow Charity Cup was an end-of-season piece of fun – albeit for very good causes. What really mattered was the glory and kudos associated with the Scottish Cup – and here Maley recalled with fondness the three previous successes of 1892, 1899 and 1900 – or the Scottish League. Maley was aware that the best team over the season won the League, and he was impressed by Rangers' strength in winning it four times in a row. Hibs were the current champions in 1903, however: perhaps Rangers had peaked. A great deal was going to depend on the youngsters, and on one in particular – Jimmy Quinn.

The 1903/04 season opened on 15 August in torrential rain, with Quinn on the left wing and Bennett in the centre, for the arrival of Partick Thistle. A competent 2-1 win was secured. It was the first game in which Celtic actually wore the horizontal stripes (a century later they would still be the same and called 'the hoops'), and somehow or other this gave the team a very youthful appearance, according to the *Glasgow Herald*. They were, of course, a very young side and noticeably enjoying their football; playing as if they wanted to be playing the game, not like people who only did it for the wages. In a very positive sense, they resembled an 'amateur' side.

Quinn was tried in the centre forward position on the Wednesday night. It was an historic occasion, but sadly not a competitive match. Celtic had been invited by Dunfermline FC for the opening of their new ground called East End Park. To the delight of Celtic, and Quinn's increasing number of admirers in Fife, Jimmy scored a hat-trick in a 5-1 romp. Maley was delighted with the play, but more so with the friendly reception that Celtic received in Dunfermline, being escorted by about thirty fans to and from the railway station.

Quinn tended to be used on the left wing for League games and indications of the success or otherwise of the season surfaced when Celtic beat Hibs 2-0 at Easter Road, and 1-0 at Parkhead, but lost to the strong-going Third Lanark (for whom Johnnie Campbell now played). Press reports of Quinn indicate a more mature and intelligent player than he had been in the last couple of seasons. 'Quinn brought brains to his play, combined with the other forwards, gone the pell-mell rushes that tired him out' was said after the 2-0 win over Hibs and, following a game against Queen's Park in the Glasgow Cup, 'Quinn last season was a daring individualist, a touchline flier, a freelance of roving and independent propensities' according to an erudite writer in the *Glasgow Herald*. 'Now he is part of the machine, a tactician, a restrained and helpful partner'.

This general improvement in the consistency of his play may well have reflected his more settled home life now that he was married, or quite simply that he got on with the young blood round about him. The team generally was playing a great deal better, and Maley had added another forward to the squad in Sam Gilligan from Dundee. Sam was not a great success, but to him goes the honour of kicking the first ball in anger on the new Hampden Park, which was opened on 31 October 1903. Sadly, Celtic seemed to find this occasion too much for them – they certainly retaliated in kind to Queen's Park's rough tactics – and lost 0-1.

Disappointment came Celtic's way at the end of November, when they lost the Glasgow Cup final in a replay to Johnnie Campbell's invigorated Third Lanark. Gilligan was injured in mid-December and Quinn found himself in the centre for Airdrie's first ever visit to Celtic Park, but Press reports are unsympathetic to the forward line of Muir, McMenemy, Quinn, Somers and Hamilton – even though the team won comfortably 3-0.

Quinn may have picked up an injury that day, but the more likely explanation is that he was 'rested' or dropped as Maley tried to find the ideal forward line. He does not reappear in a competitive game from 12 December 1903 until February 1904, but he did play in a friendly on 2 January against Corinthians. Celtic suffered two bad defeats without him. One was on Celtic's first ever visit to Airdrie's Broomfield Park – a result that rocked Scotland – but the game that made Maley think that Quinn must be recalled was a 2-1 defeat at Dens Park, Dundee on 30 January, a result that gave the initiative in the League race to Third Lanark.

Quinn had had other things to think of that January as well. On 10 January, his wife gave birth to a son, called Philip after the baby's grandfather and his uncle, and Jimmy was very aware that with an extra mouth to feed, perhaps a footballer's life with all its uncertainties might not be the best way of putting bread on the table. A miner's life, even with its dangers and drudgery, might be the best way to feed his family. He reckoned that perhaps by next year, unless something spectacular happened with Celtic, he might return to the pits and play his football on an amateur level with Smithston Albion once more. He really needed to achieve success with Celtic fairly soon, he felt, or give up professional football.

The worthy Third Lanark would win the League that year, but it was the Scottish Cup of 1904 that formed the real launching pad to Quinn's greatness. Quinn was injured in mid-February when Celtic paid a rare visit to St Bernard's at the Gymnasium Grounds in Edinburgh to win 4-0. There then followed an epic struggle to get the better of Dundee. Quinn was still injured on 20 February when Dundee drew 1-1 at Parkhead, but then 27 February saw a remarkable day at Dens Park when Quinn returned. Twenty-one thousand appeared, the 'Quinn faction' of the Celtic hordes clearly convinced that the return of Quinn would win the day for them. The game had been in some doubt, but an 8 a.m. inspection confirmed that the tie could go ahead, and a telegram was sent to Mr Maley to tell Celtic to travel.

The *Dundee Courier* has a classic comment on the financial implications of this game 'Dundee are finding what a valuable asset is an undecided Cup-tie. Like last year they have been drawing in the shekels as a result of the ties, and the end has by no means come. There is the drawback however that the spectators imagine all manner of things though there is no ground whatever for the thoughts and are apt to become tired of the business.' In this respect, the writer was surely wrong. There was, as yet, no sign of the spectators becoming tired, even though a few of them might well have indulged in a few cynical thoughts about how useful it was to teams for ties to be replayed. It would be a constant theme in Edwardian Scotland, and one that would have a tragic outcome in 1909.

This Dens Park replay was a titanic struggle, containing everything but goals. Quinn was rampant in the mud on the left of the field and the game was historically significant in that it was the first game that Maley had chosen Young, Loney and Hay as his half-back line. They had played together once before, when injuries had compelled it, but for this cup tie, Maley chose these mighty men to come together. Maley also won the toss for the venue for the third game.

That interest in the tie was still growing was shown in the massive attendance of 32,000 at Celtic Park on 5 March 1904 for the deciding game. The conditions were drier and Celtic made everybody wonder what all the fuss had been about as they hammered Dundee 5-0, with the new half-back line totally dominant. The forward line was the eccentric Muir, McMenemy, Bennett, Quinn and Hamilton – because Maley felt that Davie Hamilton was too good to be left out and he thought that Jimmy Quinn, always adaptable, would relish the inside left role. This he did, for the 'Quinn-Hamilton wheel revolved to some purpose' and Jimmy scored one of Celtic's goals 'from an impossibly tight angle'.

Two weeks later, 36,000 came to Celtic Park to see the semi-final against Third Lanark, now the most consistent team in the League and looking likely Champions. The Man of the Match was 'Sunny Jim' Young, as he was now called because of an advertisement for Force breakfast cereal, whose slogan ran 'Vigor, Vim, Perfect Trim – Force made him – Sunny Jim'. The Sunny Jim character of the advertisement was always depicted as having loads of energy, and this seemed to apply to Celtic's Jim Young. The forward line, with Quinn still at inside left, also played well. Quinn got the winning goal 'to the joy of the lieges' and indeed the 2-1 victory should have been more, for Willie Orr missed a penalty.

Quinn's star was now clearly in the ascendant. That things were now happening at Parkhead and for Quinn became clear on the following Monday when Quinn received a telegram inviting him to play for the Scottish League against the English League at Bank Street, Clayton, Manchester – the then home of Manchester United – on Monday 4 April. Sunny Jim also received a similar invitation, and Maley was delighted with the news of his two young lions. Quinn was chosen for the left wing position, even though he had recently been playing as inside left.

These games involving the Scottish League against the English League or the Irish League were very important until they fizzled out under pressure of European commitments in the early 1970s. Selection was confined to those who played for a Scottish League team – thus no

Anglo-Scots were allowed – and it was often looked upon as a stepping stone to the full international squad. The 'big' international game between Scotland and England was due to be played at Celtic Park on the following Saturday, 9 April. Bobby Templeton, now of Newcastle United, would be outside left for that match, but Quinn knew that if he played well in Manchester and if Templeton were to be injured in the meantime, then he (Quinn) would be the heir apparent.

Jimmy played competently for the Scottish League that Monday afternoon in Manchester, but sadly the English League won 2-1. It was, however, a great honour to have been picked for the Scottish League, and Quinn's heart was now set on winning a full Scottish cap. He knew that this was what his father would love: old Philip was his greatest fan, but sadly no longer in the best of health as the years of semi-starvation in Ireland and the hard work down the pits in Scotland were catching up with him. It would be a great sign of the Irish community's integration into Scottish society if Quinn could win a Scottish cap. He would not, of course, be the first of Irish extraction, but what would it do for the people of Croy!

In the meantime there was this season's international at Celtic Park. Bobby Templeton, who would one day join Celtic, obstinately refused to be injured, so Jimmy had other duties. Maley was very keen that as many Celtic players as possible should be at Celtic Park to meet the guests and help with the tasks that needed doing. Jimmy willingly volunteered, for he wanted to be as close to the international scene as he possibly could. Naturally shy, however, he did not feel confident enough to talk to all the Scottish players, although Bobby Walker of Hearts was always an easy man to get along with.

The match was poor and the conditions were awful as England squeezed home 1-0. Quinn had watched the game from the pavilion, perhaps with the lingering feeling that he could have done better than some of the ineffectual Scottish forwards. He stayed around after the match with a few other players, giving Maley help to clean out the pavilion and tidy up. It was while he was doing this, that Maley asked Quinn for a word 'on the quiet'.

Maley came straight to the point, after swearing Quinn to secrecy. He wanted Jimmy to play centre forward in next week's Scottish Cup final against Rangers at New Hampden. He said that he was slowly coming to the decision that Quinn's best position was in the action in the centre of the park. Too often he was wasted on the wing if the ball did not come to him enough. His strength would be required in the middle of the field on Saturday. Quinn nodded, glad to hear that he would at least be in the team for his third Scottish Cup final, when Maley went on 'You see, Jimmy, there is another problem as well…'

It concerned Alec Bennett. Alec had played sporadically in the centre forward position since joining the club a year ago. He was a good player and had already represented Scotland against Wales this year, but he was unsettled. Alec was a non-Catholic – something that did not in itself present a problem, but he was also a Rangers supporter – again something that need not cause difficulties, but the problem lay in that Rangers had apparently approached him and offered him terms for next year. Maley confided in Quinn that he would do his utmost to persuade Alec to remain at Celtic Park for the following season, but in the meantime he was going to leave him out of the reckoning for next Saturday's Scottish Cup final. It would be unfair on Bennett to expose him to Rangers in these circumstances. Therefore, David Hamilton would be on the left wing, Peter Somers at inside left and Jimmy in the centre. Sam Gilligan was not a bad centre – for most teams, said Maley – but this was Glasgow Celtic.

Maley then looked at Jimmy and said that he hoped next Saturday would be the start of something big for Jimmy and Celtic. He had been speaking to a few of the English officials and they had been very impressed by Quinn at Manchester in the League international. They thought that the time was not far away when Jimmy Quinn would be wearing the proper Scotland jersey, whether it be the dark blue or the Rosebery colours of yellow and pink, and whether in the centre forward position or on the left wing.

Jimmy was understandably nervous about this Scottish Cup final. He sensed that it was a very important game, both for himself and for Celtic. This was the first big game for Maley's men – those who had been gathered together by the manager and who had come of age together. The team went to Seamill Hydro on the Ayrshire coast for training and relaxation for a few days before the game. Quinn could not help marvelling at how well they all got on. It was a pleasure to be with such men as they chatted up the chambermaids (although Maley frowned on such sort of sexual fraternisation, in practice he turned a blind eye to it), charmed some of the other guests, held their nightly soirees (with

Maley's encouragement and participation) and enjoyed the good food and the training for the big match.

Such luxurious hotel life was light years away from the mines and the dreadful housing of Croy, but Quinn was very aware that he should enjoy his football life to its full extent. He knew perfectly well that an injury could happen at any time, or he could lose form, or the team could do badly and then it might be a quick, one-way ticket to the pits to eke out a much harder existence. Football was a young man's game, and one should enjoy it while one could. He had thus to a certain extent changed his tune from January, when he was dabbling with the idea of quitting full-time football.

On the social side, Quinn found the soirees a problem – for he remained a naturally shy man – but could eventually be teased into a verse or two of a Scottish song. It was not his forte, however: entertaining was more the province of the extroverts like Sunny Jim and Peter Somers, whose impersonations of Maley even had the gentleman concerned laughing. Would he be laughing come Saturday night?

It is difficult, more than a hundred years later, to imagine New Hampden at the Scottish Cup final of 1904 – the venue's first big occasion. A huge crowd of 64,323 appeared, paying a total of £1,800 for the privilege. Hampden swallowed the huge crowd without a burp: 'Discomfort is at a minimum' said the impressed scribe of the *Dundee Courier*. Normally only Scotland *v.* England internationals could attract that sort of a attendance. The crowd would probably have been less partisan than one would expect today. There would be no 'Celtic end' or 'Rangers end'. Indeed, there would be no scarves or colours – although a few youngsters might sport a green or a blue rosette. Women would be scarce and men would be well dressed, for a football match was a social occasion, and everyone would wear a bonnet.

The crowd would be generally well behaved. Violence and fights were not unknown, and indeed there was a great deal of drunkenness, but there would be nothing 'organized'. Foul language would sadly be prevalent, but very seldom would there be an offensive remark about the Pope or the Irish race – it did happen in 1904, but would only become widespread in the 1920s. Rangers, in the Edwardian era, were a respectable outfit, not yet identified with Protestantism or Orange bigotry. They were merely a big football team, and by now quite clearly the rivals, albeit friendly ones, of the Celtic.

Many of the crowd would not support either team. They supported football in general, and it is often surprising when reading of Edwardian football crowds in a Scotland *v.* England game, for example, to learn that 'England appeared to a welcoming cheer from the Scottish supporters'. Similarly, Celtic and Rangers, although each had a hardcore of diehards who followed one club or other, would also attract a large number of Glaswegians (and increasingly people from other parts of Scotland as well) who merely wanted to see a good game of football, having heard of the likes of Jimmy Quinn and wishing to see him in action.

Glasgow was thronged with visitors. There was 'tremendous animation in the city all morning – and it scarcely abated in the evening'. Fortunately, there was no real trouble, although a poor chap called Alex Cowie was 'thrown by the crowd between the carriage and the platform' at Central Station and had to be taken to hospital, and a fan called John Cunningham was knocked down and injured by a horse and cab in such a way that the cabbie was arrested for negligence. There was also the story told of the two men, both friends, knocked down by another cab while they were on their way to the game. One favoured Celtic and the other's allegiance was 'blue rather than green'. Both were only slightly injured, but were taken to hospital nevertheless, where they continued their banter over the respective merits of their teams, and insisted that they had recovered enough that they could go and see the game!

The referee was Tom Robertson of Queen's Park, and he had no neutral linesmen. Each team had to appoint a linesman; honesty was expected and, usually, provided. Cheating was considered 'infra dig', and the result was that very often club linesmen would bend over backwards to give throw-ins – or 'shies' or 'flings' as they were then called – to the other side. On this occasion, Willie Maley of Celtic and William Wilton of Rangers, two good friends, did the needful.

The teams were:
Celtic: Adams; McLeod, Orr; Young, Loney, Hay; Muir, McMenemy, Quinn, Somers, Hamilton.
Rangers: Watson; N. Smith, Drummond; Henderson, Stark, Robertson; Walker, Speedie, Mackie, Donnachie, A. Smith.

Celtic started off playing towards the Mount Florida end, against the west wind. In spite of some early pressure from Celtic, it was Rangers who went ahead through Finlay Speedie. In fact he scored twice within the first twenty minutes of the game. Both of these strikes were helped by the wind and both were preventable, with Davie Adams in the Celtic goal to blame for at least one of them.

Celtic would have been entitled to feel ill done by and lesser teams would have curled up and collapsed, but this was a fine, young, eager Celtic side. The mighty half-back line of Young, Loney and Hay took command, as Rangers' forward line virtually disappeared. Jimmy Quinn then entered the scene on his first step towards Celtic immortality. 'His first goal was worth a football enthusiast's while going a distance to see' said the Press. He picked up a ball on the halfway line, shrugged off the challenge of a few Rangers players, then kicked the ball forward between Nick Smith and Stark. The ball held up in the wind, and Quinn himself charged through between the two Rangers players to hammer past Watson. Quinn had put Celtic back in the game and, just before half-time, they were on level terms as Bobby Muir beat a few men on the right wing and crossed for Quinn to score with a first-time, unstoppable shot.

At the interval a collection was taken from the huge crowd for those injured in a cricket match! The previous August at the North Inch, Perth, in a game between Forfarshire and Perthshire, a makeshift stand had collapsed and about fifty people had been injured, some seriously. Mercifully there had been no fatalities, but some of those injured would never be able to work again – and this was in an era before the Welfare State. The collection was taken by a group of boys walking round the ground holding a sheet into which the crowd were invited to throw pennies or other coins. Although some members of the crowd derived a certain sadistic pleasure in trying to hit the gatherers, most contributed generously and a sum of over £100 was raised.

In the Celtic dressing room the mood was upbeat, but Quinn did not join in any banter. He remained static on his bench, aware that the job was not yet complete. But the initiative was now with Celtic, who had come back into the contest and now had the benefit of the stiff breeze. Time and time again Quinn 'always travelling at lightning speed' gave Stark the slip, but the elusive winner would not come, even though McMenemy and Somers kept supplying Quinn with ammunition. Quinn shot several times but goalkeeper Watson denied him, on one occasion 'staying with his arm the progress of the sphere when it seemed netbound'.

Rangers were beginning to think that they had weathered the Celtic storm and that they might earn a replay when Quinn settled the issue with less than ten minutes remaining. It was a goal not unlike the first one. This time it came from the left, with Orr and Hay both involved in the build-up before the ball came to Jimmy in the middle of the Rangers half. He simply turned and charged at the goal, shrugging off desperate tackles and being fouled repeatedly before slipping the ball past the advancing Watson.

It was a goal fit to win any cup final, and Rangers knew it. They were a well-beaten side, and Quinn would remain the only scorer of a hat-trick in a Scottish Cup final until 1972 (when Dixie Deans emulated that feat). Typical of the man, Jimmy showed little emotion. There is an account of Quinn being 'surrounded and overwhelmed' by the acclaim of his team-mates, who pummelled him and slapped him on the back, but the Croy man himself simply walked back to the centre circle, head down, smiling occasionally at his comrades. Even at full time, he shook hands with his opponents and walked stoically off to accept the plaudits of Willie Maley.

The Scottish Cup was presented in private in 1904, but Quinn apparently relaxed enough to have a drink out of the trophy. Celtic had now won the Scottish Cup four times since 1888, and a great tradition was being established. If Quinn himself was phlegmatic, that could not be said about his teammates – or indeed the Celtic support, who now had a new hero. Jimmy Quinn may have had his detractors in the past, but now he was a demigod. People on trains from Glasgow to Edinburgh would now look out of the carriage windows at Croy, hoping for a glimpse of the home of Celtic's greatest footballer.

The Press were unanimous in their praise of Celtic in general and Quinn in particular. Bennett had apparently missed the game with 'flu' – a piece of disinformation successfully peddled by Maley – but '...[Bennett] could not possibly have excelled the exhibition by Quinn... the hero of the game... Celtic's young lion'. Quinn received the same sort of adulation (to his intense embarrassment) in Scotland that Plum Warner and the English cricket team received at Victoria Station in London as they returned home from Australia with the Ashes a few days later.

The *Glasgow Observer*, admittedly an outrageously pro-Celtic newspaper, bursts into eulogy: 'Jimmy Quinn is the hero of the hour. His great feat of scoring three goals in a cup final must be almost unique. I think

Peter Dowds did something similar in the famous '92 Cup Final when the now defunct *Mail* was so chagrined by the Queen's Park defeat that it labelled the Celtic players as 'Muldoons'. Quinn's strong dashing accurate play is accentuated by his modest bearing and quiet, cool demeanour. After scoring his third goal he was nearly dismembered by the wild embraces of his mates, one of whom actually kissed the successful marksman. He himself, however, remained unmoved "Look at him" shouted an enthusiastic Celt in the reserved enclosure, "Look at him; he is as cool as hell!"'

The emotions of this writer supersede his accuracy – Dowds did not score in the 1892 Cup Final: the writer is possibly thinking of the Glasgow Cup final of 1891 – and in fact Jimmy was the first ever scorer of a hat-trick in a Scottish Cup final, if we ignore the somewhat nebulous and unsubstantiated claims of a Queen's Park man in the early years. The *Kirkintilloch Gazette*, clearly revelling in the reflected glory of a local man, quotes this passage from the *Glasgow Observer* and, a propos of the 'cool as hell' simile, states 'That comparison is novel and startling; let us hope that is also quite accurate. In those days of radium waves and liquid oxygen, nothing should surprise us'.

Jimmy had quite clearly made it, but the 1903/04 season had not yet finished. There was to be a rather nasty piece of revenge meted out to Jimmy, but in the meantime there was no stopping the boy from Croy. Five goals against a poor Kilmarnock team were followed by a couple in a meaningless Inter City League game against Rangers, and then Quinn and Celtic were off on a tour of Northern Scotland, where the team in general and he in particular were lauded in Dundee, Aberdeen and Inverness. Dundee had a large Irish population and a great welcome there was always assured, but Aberdeen and Inverness showed the ever-increasing love of the football-supporting Scotsman for the team that were always referred to as 'The Celtic'. In addition, everyone wanted to see this man who could score a hat-trick in a Scottish Cup final.

There would be more touring, for Celtic had arranged a European tour of the Austro-Hungarian Empire and Germany in Maley's attempt to spread the Celtic gospel worldwide. Quinn was never happy about being far from Croy and his beloved Annie and family, but he knew that it would be a great experience.

But there was still the Glasgow Charity Cup. In the semi-final, Quinn scored Celtic's two goals against Queen's Park at Cathkin, in a match made memorable by what happened afterwards across the city. At Parkhead, the original North Stand caught fire hours after everyone had gone home, having dropped off the kit that had been used in the Cathkin match. Whether it was arson or a smouldering cigarette no-one will ever know, although cynics were not slow to suggest that it was an 'insurance job' (the stand was somewhat rickety and increasingly unattractive for spectators). The pavilion was saved (just), but the stand would in time be replaced by the hideous building with a resemblance to a cowshed that became known as the 'Jungle' and which stayed in position until 1966 (with choking dust on hot days and holes in the roof on rainy ones) before being replaced by a slightly comelier enclosure, also called the 'Jungle'.

It was the Glasgow Charity Cup final that brought Jimmy down to earth. The game was against Rangers at Hampden on 14 May 1904, in front of 26,000 spectators. Rangers were clearly out for revenge for their Scottish Cup final defeat, not to mention endeavouring to save themselves from a trophy-less season. The game had not gone two minutes when Quinn was the victim of a hefty and high challenge from Nick Smith, which split open his thigh muscle, saw him carried off to hospital, and reduced him to a cripple until the start of the next season.

The circumstances make it hard to believe that it was a total accident, yet Smith was not sent off and indeed Celtic, without their star man, went on to lose 2-5. There were several consequences of this. One was that Quinn missed the European tour, another was that Quinn – normally the most gentlemanly and forgiving of characters – nursed a grudge against Smith and Rangers for some time after this (and did not always find it easy to control his feelings about the Ibrox club) and yet another consequence was that the Celtic supporters were given more ammunition for their paranoia complex, which even in the early days was gathering momentum.

Thus Quinn, the hero of 1904, spent the summer limping round Croy with crutches, then a stick, before eventually recovering. He was by no means a bitter man in general terms, and was far too introverted to show his emotions openly, but he did silently retain this grievance and kept his determination to make Rangers suffer. He was, of course, just the man to do that.

In the meantime he had quite a lot to be happy about. The doctors said that his leg would heal, albeit slowly. He was still earning good money. He was the hero of the Celtic-supporting fraternity – an ever growing number and now even attracting quite a few non-Irish to their ranks, especially outside Glasgow and particularly after Jimmy's famous Scottish Cup final performance. He had now won a Scottish League 'cap' and clearly had an opportunity to win full honours very soon and, as important as anything else was to Jimmy, he still retained the love and respect of the good people of Croy.

He and Annie would frequently be seen that summer with Philip in the pram and Sarah trotting alongside. The women of the village would dote over the baby, while the men would sympathise about his sore leg and talk to Jimmy about football and Celtic. No doubt there was a little jealousy now and again, for the Bible may have had a point when it said that 'a prophet is without honour in his own town'. Jimmy was, however, determined to prove it wrong. He still remained a Croy miner at heart. He had made them proud of him, but he was equally proud to be associated with them.

Jimmy was aware that there was something special about the Celtic Football Club. He knew that the very word meant Scotland and Ireland. Maley had frequently told him that this was the acceptable way for the Irish and their descendants to integrate into Scottish society. It was why Celtic Park had been built on such a huge scale, so that Scotland could play their internationals against England there. For reasons like this, the winning of a Scottish cap became very important to men like Quinn. As for Celtic, the fact that a Scottish honour had been won for the first time in four years meant that the team now had a taste of success. They wanted more. Maley and the supporters felt they had cause for optimism, but they can have had no idea how much success was soon to come their way.

FOUR

QUINN:
VILLAIN OR VICTIM?

Quinn, being a quick healer, missed only one game at the start of the 1904/05 season. He marked his return with a hat-trick over a poor Port Glasgow team on 27 August 1904, but the quality of the opposition was irrelevant. It was the fact that Quinn scored a hat-trick that appeared on all the billboards of Scotland and terrified the opposition – reminding friend and foe alike of last year's Scottish Cup final. Maley was aware that Celtic had not won the League Championship since 1898, and a seven-year gap was unacceptable to a club of Celtic's support and expectations, as he kept telling his players. With the charismatic Quinn back leading the forward line, he knew that Celtic must be one of the favourites.

Rangers were possibly now a spent force, Maley reckoned, and the current champions Third Lanark, although a fine side, looked like one-season wonders. From Edinburgh, Hibs would always be a force to reckon with, as indeed would be Hearts, as long as Bobby Walker and Charlie Thomson were around. Indeed, it was Hearts who were the first to beat Celtic on the Edinburgh Monday Holiday of 19 September 1904.

Celtic had just had a rumbustious game with St Mirren on the Saturday, in the established tradition of such encounters. As a clear sign of the growth of interest in the game among the Celtic faithful, thousands had descended on Paisley, mainly in horse-drawn brakes with names like 'The Shamrock', 'The Emeralds', 'The Charles Stuart Parnell' and one with 'The Jimmy Quinn' painted on one side and 'The Hat-trick' on the other! Love Street had probably never seen such a big crowd (looking to be well over 10,000), and the St Mirren players, far from being over-awed, attacked the game with relentless ferocity.

Celtic won 3–2. It was comfortable enough after Quinn scored twice in the first half (St Mirren's second goal came very late), but the game degenerated into a rough house. Quinn was, of course, singled out for violent treatment. The remarkable thing was that he took it all without retaliation as long as it was directed at himself. It was when Tom Jackson committed a bad foul on Quinn's friend, Jimmy McMenemy (who had special talent but little bulk), that he took action. Quinn bundled Jackson off the park when the pair of them went for a ball, and he was spoken to by the referee: 'Quinn's questionable style of deportment on the field will yet lead to trouble' says the prophetic *Glasgow Herald*.

Celtic, nursing a few injuries, then travelled to Edinburgh to play Hearts. Celtic underperformed in this match. Hearts, inspired by Bobby Walker, were quite simply the better team on the day and Quinn, with at least two men marking him, failed to make any impact. It was an experience, however, from which this young Celtic team would learn.

An important early success of the 1904/05 season was achieved in the Glasgow Cup, bringing Quinn his first medal in this competition. A comprehensive victory over Queen's Park – a team who had obstinately refused to turn professional and who suffered as a result – was followed by another fine performance against Partick Thistle to set up a final against Rangers at Hampden on 8 October.

A key character in this game was Alec Bennett. Alec, as the astute reader will recall, was dropped from the Scottish Cup final in April because of his perceived Rangers inclinations. For the meantime, he had been talked into remaining at Parkhead by Maley. Alec, a gentleman, had been shocked by the injury to Quinn in last season's Charity Cup final and had decided to stay at Celtic Park. Quinn, as was his wont, went out of his way to befriend him and to let him know that, although they had been rivals for a first-team spot, there was nothing personal. Just at the right time Maley found a slot for Alec on the right wing, so the mighty forward line of Bennett, McMenemy, Quinn, Somers and Hamilton now took shape. Arguably, it was the best in the history of the club. That statement can never be proved, but what is beyond doubt is that it was the finest in Edwardian Scotland.

A crowd of 55,000 – almost as many as the previous season's Cup Final – assembled at Hampden to see the battle of the giants. It was a fine game, but Celtic deserved their 2-1 victory. They went down to an early goal, but then Quinn was on hand to equalize. After half-time, Quinn fed Bennett to put Celtic ahead, and then the mighty men of Young, Loney and Hay 'closed the game down at the halfway line'. Willie Loney gobbled up everything that came down the middle, and on the odd time that Rangers got through, Davie Adams (now over any crisis of confidence he might have had following his mistakes in last season's Scottish Cup final) saved brilliantly.

The following week Celtic and Rangers drew at Parkhead in a League match in front of 30,000, and then Quinn scored twice against Third Lanark at Cathkin Park in a game rendered remarkable by an injury to the referee and Third Lanark's protestations about his replacement! Apparently, a man from the crowd came forward when the referee was injured and said that he had done such a job before. Both sides agreed at the time, but then Thirds, having lost the game, wanted a replay. They were ruled out of order because there was no perceived alternative to this mysterious man at the time.

Celtic finished 1904 undefeated in the League, apart from that blemish at Tynecastle in September. Injuries to McMenemy compelled a shuffling of the forward line, with Quinn often at inside left and Harry McIlvenny (who had played for the club some seven years previously and had now been brought back) at centre forward. McIlvenny was not a total success, but the team kept performing well with Quinn, although quite clearly a centre forward, capable of performing elsewhere in the forward line.

Quinn was never a selfish player. He was very much a team man, being too modest and shy to be a seeker of the limelight at the expense of anyone else. He was a great encourager, and also a protector of his teammates – telling brutal opposing defenders, for example, that another foul on a comrade would mean that 'ye wad hae me tae answer tae!' You did not take liberties with a man of Quinn's build. Celtic reached New Year four points clear of Rangers, although Rangers had a game in hand.

Quinn, however, was injured for the 1905 New Year's Day game at Ibrox. He thus probably did well to miss a game that had to be abandoned in the second half because of the constant encroachment of fans. Sixty thousand had paid to get in, but several more thousands had rushed the primitive gates or scaled the inadequate walls, such was the interest in the game.

A few days after this, on 6 January 1905, an extraordinary event occurred which shook Quinn. His old adversary Nick Smith, who had injured him the previous May, died of the enteric fever that was ravaging Ayrshire (where Smith lived) and that had claimed the life of his wife a few days previously. Scottish football was devastated, but Quinn could not go along entirely with the grief that he was expected to show.

Quinn knew that some people would say 'It's all in the game' and 'You have to be able to take it' and 'Scottish football is no place for softies'. He was also aware that his own men could dish out the raw meat as well. He knew that Willie Loney and Willie Orr took no prisoners and, very soon, Sunny Jim would be suspended for a month for kicking a Partick Thistle player. But Quinn did feel that Smith's foul on him in the Glasgow Charity Cup final was a deliberate attempt early in the game to knock him out of contention and reduce Celtic to ten men. There was also an element of revenge and no little spite involved.

In this attempt at dirty play, Smith succeeded, and Quinn had resented it bitterly, but death had removed Smith from the equation forever. It is sometimes difficult to cope with one's emotions at the news of the death of someone one does not like. There was little more that Quinn could do now, however, other than to feel sorry for the demise of a fellow footballer. Any outpouring of emotion would have been hypocrisy.

Quinn came back from injury to play at inside left with Bennett in the centre at Dens Park on 14 January 1905. The pitch was hard and only just playable, but that does not excuse Celtic's feeble performance in a 1-2 defeat. It did, however, concentrate Maley's mind about Quinn. There must be an end to this uncertainty. If Quinn were to play at all in future (and he could hardly now be omitted for reasons other than injury), it really would have to be in the centre forward position where he could use his strength, hard running and sheer determination to maximum effect.

The defeats at Dundee and against Airdrie (when Quinn was out injured) meant that Celtic had lost ground and now seemed unlikely to win the League in 1904/05. From this point, however, Celtic turned on the style and won their four remaining League games with tremendous flair and panache. Quinn was on form and scoring regularly. This was particularly true of the game at Ibrox on 18 February – the replay of the game that had been abandoned after the crowd encroachment on New Year's Day. Celtic won 4-1, and the forward line was praised in *The Scotsman* for 'putting a dash into their work which delighted their supporters and at times completely enervated the home defence as Quinn, Hamilton and Bennett led the attack in fine style.'

This was traditional Scottish forward play at its best, with Celtic's front line looking like a 'W'. The three prongs of Bennett, Quinn and Hamilton would advance in parallel formation while the inside men, McMenemy and Somers, would supply the ammunition. With the half-back line (including Alec McNair, who was deputising for the suspended Sunny Jim), taking a stranglehold on the midfield, there was little that Rangers could do. Rangers, with the wind and rain behind them in the first half, went in at the interval on level terms, but were swept aside remorselessly in the second half. Quinn scored twice, one coming from a square pass by Alec Bennett and the other a 'head-down charge up the field to score magnificently'.

The month of February 1905 saw another tragic death, and this one Jimmy felt keenly. Celtic's great Barney Battles died very suddenly in the Gallowgate of a dose of flu, still some months short of his thirtieth birthday. Quinn was shocked by this one, for Barney, a tough and crusty character who had had several well-publicised spats with Maley and the Celtic Establishment, had been very kind to Jimmy when he joined the club. The shy Quinn had always been very grateful for the fact that the great Barney Battles, for all his apparent sullenness and unsociability, had gone out of his way to make the youngster feel welcome.

Battles had lost his place to Willie Orr and was now with Kilmarnock. Indeed he had played twice against Celtic that year, the latest being on Hogmanay. Dalbeth Cemetery on Sunday 12 February saw a crowd of 40,000, with Scottish football well represented. It was four Celtic men who carried the coffin. Although Barney had played for quite a few clubs and had been capped 3 times for Scotland in 1901, he was always Barney Battles of Celtic. Quinn made a point of talking to his distressed widow, who would be presented with the stand takings for the Scotland v. Ireland international on 18 March, a week after a special friendly benefit game between Celtic and Kilmarnock. She was, in fact, pregnant with another Barney Battles, who would play for Hearts and Scotland in the future.

The month of March would also be very significant for Quinn. He would reach the heights and scale the depths, and his name, which was already in common currency throughout Scotland, would now reverberate to an even greater extent. Celtic played their last League game at Motherwell on 4 March and won 6-2. Quinn scored a hat-trick, even though he was seen to limp for a great part of the game after a hefty challenge. This now meant that Celtic could not be beaten in the League race. Rangers could, however, equal them if they won their two games in hand. How that would be resolved, no-one yet knew. It would presumably mean a play-off, for goal average or goal difference had not yet been thought of.

But the following two weeks would see Quinn in a different colour of jersey. He won his second 'League' cap at Hampden on 11 March against the English League in a forward line of Bennett (Celtic), Walker (Hearts), Quinn (Celtic), Speedie (Rangers) and Smith (Rangers). The game finished 2-2, and Quinn scored one of the Scottish League's goals after two fine one-twos involving his excellent inside men Bobby Walker and Findlay Speedie. The *Dundee Courier* is ambivalent about Quinn, saying 'Quinn played with any amount of dash and had several fine tries but some of his finishes lacked judgement'.

By the Monday, all Croy was alight with the news that Jimmy Quinn had been awarded his first full Scotland cap. It was against Ireland (of all people) at Celtic Park (of all places) on Saturday 18 March 1905, and Jimmy would hardly be alone, for MacLeod, Hay, McMenemy and Somers of Celtic would also be in the Scottish team.

Quinn's father was delighted. Here at last was proof that his family had made it. His son was playing for Scotland against Ireland. Old Philip would go to the game (he normally now went to as many as he could in any case) and the fact that it was for his new country against his old country would not matter. Football had been slow in starting in Ireland and tended to be played mainly among the Protestant community in the north, but the game was expanding southwards as well. Not that it mattered: Jimmy was undeniably Scottish, and the family must therefore support him. In any case, the 'big' international was against England at Crystal Palace on 1 April. Jimmy, if he played well against Ireland, would have a good chance of being picked for that one.

The weather was not kind on 18 March, but 37,000 appeared at Celtic Park to see Scotland win 4-0. Quinn scored the third goal after a fine through-ball from Bobby Walker of Hearts, and he had every reason to be pleased with his performance. At half-time, a man had appeared with sandwich boards advertising a railway trip to London on 1 April. Jimmy would surely be hoping that half of Croy would treat themselves to a trip to the capital to see him playing against England.

The team would be announced on Monday 27 March, but in the meantime Celtic had a rather important fixture on the Saturday before in the shape of a Scottish Cup semi-final against Rangers at Parkhead. They had reached that stage by defeating Dumfries, Lochgelly and Partick Thistle, and such had been their dominance of Rangers on 18 February in the Scottish League fixture, that they had no reason to fear the Ibrox men.

Once again, the weather was bad, and 35,000 saw a dull game until things became 'very animated in the latter stages'. That was putting it very mildly. Donnie MacLeod, Celtic's right-back, was badly injured before half-time, and thus Celtic had to play in heavy conditions in the second half with only ten men. Speedie put Rangers ahead midway through the second half, and then with time running out and Celtic looking likely to equalize, Rangers broke through and goalkeeper Adams continued his melancholy tradition of making mistakes against Rangers by dropping the slippery ball and allowing Robertson to score.

Inside the last ten minutes, with only ten men and two goals down, Celtic were in a situation that would be difficult to recover from. With their mighty forward line and fanatical support cheering them on, however, anything remained possible. A high ball came into the goalmouth and Rangers' left-back, Alec Craig, slipped on the wet turf, fell and – to break his fall – grabbed hold of Quinn's leg. Quinn shook the limb to escape such unwelcome, if accidental, attentions and in so doing his foot came into contact with Craig's face.

Referee Tom Robertson of Queen's Park who had already spoken to Quinn for his 'attentions to the goalkeeper' thought that this was a deliberate kick. He immediately sent Quinn off, even though Craig himself tried to intervene on Quinn's behalf. Quinn, though protesting his innocence, trudged off the pitch, feeling that life was against him. The team with only nine men had now surely lost the game. He had been wrongly sent off, and with this incident had gone not only the Scottish Cup but also had imperilled his own chance, presumably, of winning a Scottish cap against England.

As he reached the pavilion, he heard a noise. He turned round to see that a few youngsters had scaled the spiked palings and had invaded the pitch in protest at what they saw as a gross injustice. A few Rangers players were jostled and then someone threw a punch at the referee as he tried to run off with the rest of the players to escape the crowd. After a few minutes (in which some Rangers players came up to Quinn to say that Mr Robertson had made a mistake) the players went back on the field, minus Quinn of course, but the game could not restart because of a further encroachment.

Celtic would nobly concede the game to Rangers. Indeed, with only nine men and two goals down, they had little chance of squaring things in the remaining seven minutes or so. This was accepted by their supporters who would concede in a weak moment that Rangers had played well that day. It was what later happened with Jimmy Quinn that was unacceptable, and indeed gave food for an early example of what has come to be known as 'The Celtic Paranoia'.

The unfortunate scenes at the end tended to cloud judgement on the crucial point of whether or not Quinn kicked a Rangers player. Hysteria was fanned by the newspapers, and Celtic were portrayed as a bunch of fouling players and violent fans. Some of this was due to pre-existing anti-Irish or anti-Catholic prejudice, but what made matters worse was that this concerned the 'man of the moment' in Jimmy Quinn. One recalls the sheer volume of media coverage in 1998 when David Beckham was sent off in a World Cup match against Argentina. All sorts of extraneous information about the Falklands War and the 1966 World Cup was brought up. Something similar happened with Quinn in 1905. All sorts of silly things were said and written about Fenian bombings and the Irish taking over Scotland, etc. Such was the atmosphere in the country that justice on the key point was not likely to be given.

Quinn's case was heard on Wednesday 29 March. The Scotland team had already been picked on the Monday and Quinn's name was not on the list. Quinn had thus already lost a great deal by the time of the hearing. Quinn, being a shy man and already enjoying the nickname of 'Jamie the Silent', would not have made a good case in his own defence, but he submitted a letter, as indeed did the honest Alec Craig – who stated categorically that 'Quinn neither kicked nor stamped on me'. Rangers centre half Stark also backed Quinn up.

In spite of this, the Disciplinary Committee of the SFA endorsed the decision of referee Tom Robertson, and Quinn was suspended for a month. Two weeks later, on 11 April, he appealed, but his appeal was also rejected. This time we are told that it was by a majority of 13-10, clearly showing that a substantial minority were now becoming convinced that an injustice had been done. But there were still not enough to exonerate Jimmy.

Thus 'Jamie the Silent' became 'Jamie the Sullen' during the month of April. In a sense he did not miss very much other than his international cap, for Celtic had no fixtures left other than in the irrelevant Glasgow League, which was largely ignored by the fans. Rangers were in business, however. To the horror of their fans, they lost the Scottish Cup final to Third Lanark, and on the day that Quinn played his first game after suspension (29 April), Rangers beat Morton 2-0 to draw level with Celtic at the top of the Scottish League.

Had goal average or goal difference been in vogue, Rangers would have won the League, but it was decided that the Glasgow League game between the two clubs scheduled for Saturday 6 May would double as the Scottish League decider. Given the circumstances of the Scottish Cup semi-final, a decision was made to appoint an English referee, namely Mr Kirkham of Preston. He had little bother, for on a coldish but dry day in front of a surprisingly small crowd of 30,000 at Hampden Park, Celtic won their first League title since 1898 by beating Rangers 2-1. The forwards all 'played with dash' – a very common description in the 1900s newspapers – and although Quinn did not score, he was instrumental in the build-up to McMenemy's soft mishit shot which deceived goalkeeper Tommy Sinclair, and it was Quinn who passed to Hamilton on the left wing to score with a speculative lob. In view of what had happened the last time, Maley had given strict instructions to all, especially Quinn, to be on their best behaviour. The occasion passed peacefully, the only unfortunate occasion being when Rangers' right half Gourlay was taken off after an accidental clash with Quinn.

Full time saw an unleashing of joy from the Celtic-minded among the supporters that paralleled that of the previous year's Scottish Cup final. The hugging and kissing of complete strangers when a team scores is common enough nowadays, but normally in 1905 one would have confined oneself to polite applause and possibly even the raising of a cap in appreciation. The *Glasgow Observer*, an unashamed, unrepentant and occasionally bigoted devotee of the Celtic cause tells stories of grown men weeping for joy, embracing their neighbours and even dancing on the cinder track, all the while singing 'songs of their childhood'.

The capture of the League Championship of 1905 mollified Quinn to a certain extent. He felt that over the season Celtic had played the better football than Rangers, and that the possession of the League Championship trophy and his own personal medal (and the one he won in the Glasgow Cup) proved this. He still felt unjustly treated and would continue to do so all his life over what happened in the semi-final, but reckoned that the breaks tended to level themselves out. There remained in 1905 the Glasgow Charity Cup, and this too found its way to Celtic Park as Celtic beat Queen's Park 3-0 and Partick Thistle 2-0.

It was thus an excellent season, with Celtic winning three out of the four major trophies available to them. Quinn had won a League cap and a full cap, so apart from 25 March, everything was reasonably rosy. There remained a curious sequel to the Quinn/Craig affair. Quinn, with the backing of Celtic, sued the *Glasgow Evening News* newspaper for saying that Quinn had been guilty of 'violent play', and that he had 'brutally and savagely kicked' Craig. Oddly, it was a case of slander, although normally anything written down is libel. The newspaper, in its defence, claimed that the SFA had backed up the referee on two occasions (the hearing and the appeal) and therefore it was reasonable to assume that Quinn was indeed guilty of 'violent play'. The court of law on 16 November 1905 demurred, and awarded the case to Quinn – although the award was hardly a ring-ing endorsement of Jimmy's innocence. He had claimed £500, but the damages were set at a single shilling and no costs were awarded. Quinn, nevertheless, felt himself to a certain extent vindicated.

This case attracted a great deal of publicity – something that might have once upset the shy Jimmy Quinn. But any chance of Quinn leading the life of a recluse had long gone. Quinn was the name that was talked about throughout Scotland. The rival papers of the *Glasgow Evening News* gloated in the misfortune of that institution and milked the story all they could.

By the time the case came up, Celtic had started the 1905/06 season well. The Glasgow Cup was already on the shelf after convincing wins over Queen's Park, Partick Thistle and Third Lanark, and without a goal being lost. The final against Third Lanark on 7 October at Hampden was played in heavy rain, and Quinn opened the scoring with a twenty-yard drive so fierce that the ball hit the back of the net and came out again.

League form was also good, with only five points being dropped before the New Year. One was a draw at Tynecastle with Hearts, while two points were dropped in gut-wrenching circumstances at Ibrox when

Rangers scored with almost the last kick. Still less acceptable was the loss to Port Glasgow in the rain at Parkhead. It was a game that showed how much Celtic needed Jimmy Quinn, for Quinn (whose wife had given birth to his third child Catherine in midweek) was injured early on and had a very quiet match. Port Glasgow's goalkeeper played the game of his life, and Celtic, with a less than totally fit Quinn, simply could not score.

But this was a very competitive League, with Airdrie also doing well. When the Diamonds came to Parkhead in late September, a crowd of 35,000 appeared. Some of them got in for nothing, for they broke down the wooden exit gate and charged in. Quinn was at inside left that day, as Peter Somers was injured and Maley put Bennett at centre forward and brought Alec McNair forward to the right wing position. The *Glasgow Observer* says that Quinn was 'tearing like a tiger' all game and turns to a Homeric simile to tell its readers how the injured Peter Somers saw the game. In the *Iliad*, King Priam of Troy would frequently take his place on the battlements to watch the fray between his Trojans and the Greeks, expressing by groans, sighs and gestures his emotions on what was happening. In like fashion, apparently, did Somers on the pavilion balcony show his feelings, although he would have been glad at the end, for Celtic won 2-1.

On 30 December Celtic ensured that they would finish 1905 at the top of the League when they beat Hibs at Easter Road. The game was petering out, and a mediocre Hibs side looked as if they had done enough to deny Celtic a deserved victory, when in the eighty-seventh minute a through-ball found Quinn, who hammered it home first time with his lethal left foot.

It was in some ways a typical Quinn goal. Jimmy was a centre forward who believed in shooting. He knew that when a ball comes to a forward, particularly if it is within the penalty area, a first-time shot has a far better chance of success than any attempt to play about with the ball and to round the goalkeeper. He did have some misses, but that has to be accepted. On this occasion his aim was true, and the talk on the trains back from Edinburgh to Glasgow that Saturday night was of little other than Jimmy Quinn.

Quinn himself and the rest of the Celtic party travelled back to Glasgow on a later train once the majority of the support had gone. Those supporters on that train would have a chance to see their heroes and to talk to them, for Maley was always keen to encourage that sort of thing. He would also be the first to intervene if he thought that any of the fans were becoming too much of a nuisance, and sometimes this involved 'protecting' Jimmy Quinn. Jimmy remained a shy, introverted man who did not find it easy to chat with fans in the way that Sunny Jim or Jimmy McMenemy did. He would nod politely, but only very seldom would he say much.

In fact it became a cliché among the support that Quinn looked just like an ordinary man. One would not think that he was the idol of the team and the most talked-about man in Scotland. When the Edinburgh train that night reached Croy Station, Quinn collected his bag and disembarked to head down the road back to his beloved Annie and family.

Celtic would duly continue their progress towards their second successive League Championship in the early months of 1906. It was an exciting time to be alive, for in early January, a Liberal Government had been returned with a huge majority under the leadership of Glaswegian Prime Minister Sir Henry Campbell-Bannerman. Scotland traditionally voted Liberal in those days, and much was expected of the Liberals in terms of social reform. They would not entirely disappoint, and made what was at least a start in addressing the horrendous problems of poverty that had been around since the Industrial Revolution of almost a hundred years ago.

Celtic beat Rangers at Parkhead on New Year's Day 1906, then recorded fine victories over Kilmarnock, Falkirk and Airdrie. Oddly enough, in the 7-0 thrashing of Falkirk, Quinn did not score, but he made up for it the following week by notching a fine hat-trick at Broomfield against Airdrie, injuring himself in the undertaking and missing the next game.

At the end of January and beginning of February, Celtic went to Dundee two weeks in succession. Thirty thousand (including a massive 10,000 from Glasgow) packed Dens Park for a cup tie and saw Celtic win in controversial circumstances. For Celtic's first goal, a corner from Alec Bennett saw Quinn, Somers and Dundee's Henderson rise for the ball, and it ended up in the net. It is generally described as an own goal by Henderson, but Dundee fans were convinced that Quinn or Somers punched the ball off Henderson's shoulder into the net. After Dundee equalized, however, there was little doubt about Celtic's second and decisive goal, as Quinn released Somers with a brilliant through-ball.

Once again Quinn was injured in this game and missed the League match the following week between the same two sides. Celtic lost this one, as indeed they would lose at Aberdeen a month later – the common factor being that Quinn was not playing.

There was no such excuse for the defeat by Hearts in the Scottish Cup. On 24 February, an astonishingly large crowd of 50,000 (including many from Edinburgh) assembled at Parkhead on a cold frosty day to see Celtic go down 1-2 to Hearts. Quinn did not score that day and indeed was well policed by Charlie Thomson, but the team in general played badly on the hard and heavily sanded pitch. Celtic might have snatched an equalizer, but it was one of these days (one of the very few days in the early 1900s) when Maley simply had to hold up his hands and say that the opposition were simply the better team. Indeed, the Edinburgh men would go on to win the Scottish Cup that year, beating Third Lanark in the final.

If Celtic were disappointed in the Scottish Cup, they had every cause to be happy with the way that they clinched the Scottish League on 10 March with two games to spare. At Hampden Park (where by coincidence they had won the Championship in 1905 as well) Celtic thrashed Queen's Park 6-0. Quinn was absolutely rampant that day, scoring four goals and being denied by the woodwork and the goalkeeper on many other occasions. His fans loved all this, and the poor performance that had seen them dumped out of the Scottish Cup a fortnight previously was forgotten and forgiven.

In actual fact, Celtic might have won the Scottish League a week previously on 3 March, but they managed to lose to Aberdeen in what was their first-ever League visit to Pittodrie. The key factor of course, according to the sages from Croy, was the absence of Jimmy Quinn, who was on international duty that day.

Jimmy in fact did not have a happy day either, as Scotland went down 0-2 to Wales at Tynecastle. It was a very fine Welsh team who had beaten Scotland the previous year as well, but this defeat went down particularly badly for it was the first time that Wales had won in Scotland. The crowd was massive, possibly too big for Tynecastle, but they were grievously disappointed with Scotland's defensive and goalkeeping errors – and also the substandard performance of Quinn who 'missed the few chances that came his way' according to the grief-stricken writer of *The Scotsman*.

In spite of his poor showing against Wales, Quinn was given another bite at the international cherry. This was against Ireland at Dalymount Park, Dublin. The venue was a surprise, for although Scotland also played there two years ago, attendances and interest tended to be higher in Belfast, where there was more Scottish influence. Quinn's parents were naturally delighted that Jimmy was being given the opportunity to visit the land of their birth, and appropriately, the game was to be played on St Patrick's Day, 17 March.

The team travelled by train to Liverpool and then by ship to Ireland. Quinn enjoyed the voyage, and also the opportunity to see Dublin. Not surprisingly, he was well known there, playing as he did for Glasgow Celtic, although football was by no means the obsession in Dublin that it was in Glasgow.

The Cameron Highlanders were there and their band entertained the crowd at half-time with Scottish and Irish songs. Quinn would notice also that the soldiers of the Cameron Highlanders were present as a low-key but nonetheless still visible presence. The Fenians had been quiet for some time now, but the continuing failure of the British Government to deliver Irish Home Rule was a constant sore point with the Irish. St Patrick's Day and the presence of the famous Scotland football team might have been an opportunity for the terrorists to assert their position.

Fortunately, the crowd was well behaved and no political point was made. It was in fact a fairly disappointing game that Scotland won 1-0, the goal being scored by the eccentric amateur Tommy Fitchie of Arsenal. Quinn had a good game in his third full international, and although he did not score, he nurtured hopes that he might be playing in the Scotland *v*. England match at Hampden Park on 7 April.

He was certainly picked for the 'League international' against the English League for the third year in a row. This was played the week after the Dublin game and once again Quinn (with Celtic teammates Sunny Jim Young and Donnie MacLeod) was invited to travel. This time it was to London and Stamford Bridge, the home of Chelsea, for a game that was played in front of 20,000. The Scottish League played disastrously and lost 2-6. Donnie MacLeod retained his place for the 'big' international, but Quinn and Sunny Jim were held responsible and dropped, Quinn's place going to Alec Menzies of Hearts.

Quinn and his supporters felt that this was unfair, and the *Glasgow Herald* was adamant that Quinn would have done a great deal better if he had had better inside forwards than Walker and Kyle. Walker had a particularly bad day, and Kyle's only contribution had been the first goal, which came after a pass from Quinn. Quinn had also been unlucky and at one point hit the post with a powerful shot. In addition, he had been up against an inspired goalkeeper in Ashcroft of Woolwich Arsenal.

Quinn's friends sensed conspiracies and plots against him, but the edge was taken off their objection when Scotland (in front of a truly massive crowd of well over 100,000) beat England 2-1 at Hampden Park. It was, nevertheless, another example of the Quinn persecution complex – something that owed little to Quinn himself, but was a key factor in the metabolism of the Quinn fan club. There was, of course, no such body in any official sense, but unofficially it contained all Celtic supporters and quite a few adherents from other teams as well who believed (often quite irrationally) that Quinn was somehow picked upon.

The season now fizzled out. Celtic were the League Champions, comfortably and deservedly. It was clear that a great team was now in place at Celtic Park – a team worthy of the massive stadium that they had. Interest in football in Scotland had rocketed over the past twenty years, and this had been due on no small measure to the Celtic side with their massive support, and their ability to galvanise the interests and energies of an otherwise dispossessed and underprivileged ethnic minority.

The great thing about this team was their ability to attract the support and admiration of people who were not themselves Irish or Catholic, a phenomenon that was especially marked in the east of the country. When Celtic went to Dundee, for example, people would flock to see the 'Bould Celts' which included Jimmy Quinn (or sometimes simply to see Jimmy Quinn). Arguments about football could often be settled with the claim 'Look, I've seen Jimmy Quinn'.

One of the factors that marked Celtic was that they played the game as if they wanted to play it. They enjoyed their football, ran about for each other and generally played with a passion that frequently had sports writers lapsing into French to describe it: thus we often find '*joie de vivre*', '*élan*' and '*panache*' – as well as the more pedestrian '*savoir faire*' – being used by plaudits when they attempt to evoke the side. Against the elegant Celts, said *The Scotsman* on one occasion, it is a case of '*sauve qui peut*'.

Yet in 1906, the team, though outstanding and quite clearly the best in Scotland and arguably in Britain as well, was not yet the finished article. The defeat in the Scottish Cup quarter-final to Hearts had hurt, as indeed would the loss in the Glasgow Charity Cup to Rangers on 5 May (a defeat only partly to be explained away by the absence of Sunny Jim). The *Glasgow Herald* says that 'Quinn and McMenemy were the best Celtic forwards without however touching the effective standard of any of the opposing five'. It was a sad end to the competitive season, but there were so many other good things going on that spring as well.

For example, Bradford and Bolton both had the opportunity to see the mighty Quinn, as indeed did the Highlands – for Maley was always keen to teach the world the Celtic gospel. Each game played always attracted a large crowd of locals, eager to see the mighty men, especially that Quinn that everyone talked about, and was invariably recalled (with occasional fictitious additions) in local folklore for generations afterwards.

The game at Valley Parade, Bradford in particular on Easter Monday saw Quinn scoring two goals in front of an awestruck home crowd and 300 Glasgow supporters who had travelled to see them. The supporters were raucous, drunken and vociferous, but endeared themselves to the locals by their good nature and willingness to share out their alcohol and to entertain them with their wide repertoire of Irish and Scottish songs whenever the game got boring.

The main event for Quinn, however, was the tour of central Europe in late May and early June 1906 when he played games in Hamburg, Leipzig, Berlin, Prague and Budapest. It will be recalled that the previous trip in 1904 took place without Quinn, who was recovering from Nick Smith's vicious tackle. Quinn, never a great traveller and a man who often said of himself that he 'got homesick on the train from Croy to Glasgow', was nevertheless the same kind of hero in Central Europe as he was in Scotland, scoring freely – notably his five goals in Leipzig. Some of the games were rough and on substandard, primitive pitches. Quinn is reported as having been 'badly knocked about' in a game in Berlin against some unsophisticated Germans. It did not, however, stop him from scoring two goals that day.

His return home on 6 June marked the end of five-and-a-half years with Celtic. He was still a couple of years short of his thirtieth birthday and had a great deal left in him. He loved his team, their supporters, his teammates and even the sometimes irascible and unpredictable Maley. He had won the Scottish League twice, the Scottish Cup once and both

Glasgow tournaments on various occasions. He had been capped for Scotland against Ireland and Wales, although not yet against England, and he was undeniably the most talked-about man in Scottish football circles. Whenever anyone mentioned Croy, someone would invariably say 'That's where Quinn lives'.

He had several regrets. One was the constant injuries and the long-term damage that was being done to his legs by ferocious tackles from defenders who could stop him in any other way. The other was that he still had not played for Scotland against England – something that he was determined to do, for that was the important game in those days.

For Jimmy there was an awful lot, both good and bad, to come. He spent the rest of the summer of 1906 quietly with his family, keeping himself fit with runs around Croy and Kilsyth. Like most men who are shy and socially insecure in a cosmopolitan set-up, there was no problem for Jimmy in his own background. He would speak to everyone he met, even on occasion treating himself to the odd drink ('as long as ye prom-ise no tae tell Maley') with his friends. He would not have been able to do this very easily in Croy, of course, for it was a 'dry' village, as indeed was Kilsyth from time to time, but there were always ways and means…

Quinn could certainly not be accused of being big-headed, even though he was now one of the most famous men in Scotland. Generally speaking, everyone in Croy supported Celtic, but even the Rangers sup-porters in Kilsyth loved the unassuming Celt, arguing amiably with him when they saw him about who was to win next year's Scottish Cup.

There certainly seemed to be little chance of anyone other than Celtic lifting the League of 1907. They reached New Year without losing a game, a remarkable feat when one considers that they had to do this with serious injuries to goalkeeper Davie Adams, centre half Willie Loney and left half Jimmy Hay. It is a tribute to the team that the reserves fitted in seamlessly – but of course there was always the man up front who could be relied upon to score almost impossible goals that no other mortal could have.

The goalkeeping situation was remarkable and dealt with in a way that simply would not happen 100 years later. Davie Adams injured his hand on a nail while playing in a benefit match for Finlay Speedie of Rangers. Rangers felt guilty about this and offered their reserve goalkeeper, Tommy Sinclair, to Celtic. Maley gladly accepted and Sinclair played 9 games for

Celtic and only conceded 2 goals – both of them in the Glasgow Cup final against Third Lanark. Sinclair was vexed at himself about losing his impeccable record, but his anger was mollified when Celtic won and he collected a winners' medal before returning to Ibrox!

Willie Loney broke his arm against Hearts on 15 September 1906. For a while reserve Alec Wilson was used, but then the ever-versatile Eck McNair was deployed. When Jimmy Hay was injured, he was immediately replaced by the grossly underrated Johnny Mitchell. The team continued with hardly a hiccup, and the talk of all Scotland was the form of the forward line of Bennett, McMenemy, Quinn, Somers and Hamilton – a strike force whose efficiency was hardly impaired when Bobby Templeton occasionally took over from David Hamilton.

Quinn scored three hat-tricks (against Hamilton, Motherwell and St Mirren) and scored twice on at least five occasions. It was noticeable that the one game in which Celtic did not score was at Dens Park, Dundee on 20 October. Why was that? Quinn was out with an ankle strain, and it was also the game that Hay was carried off early with a broken collarbone!

On the day that Loney was injured, Celtic still beat Hearts 3-0 with the triumphant *Glasgow Observer* noting that 'the stands rose as one man to greet Quinn's goal'. At Broomfield on 29 September, Quinn had already scored once and then hit a shot 'with a force that well-nigh burst the net' and as a result a brake club returned to Glasgow that night with 'Airdrie 0 Celtic 2' chalked on the side. Against Clyde in a game where Celtic struggled, it was Quinn who rescued them with a last-minute equalizer and on Hogmanay, Quinn scored the winner 'on all fours and under total pressure' against a brutal Airdrie team.

By the turn of the year Celtic had played 19 League games, won 16 and drawn 3. They had also lifted the Glasgow Cup, Quinn scoring a goal with a back-heel in the semi-final against Queen's Park and the team coming from behind against Third Lanark in the final at Ibrox. It was, of course, Quinn who equalized and set up Somers for the winner. Midwinter in 1906/07 saw much snow. In spite of that, Celtic played Woolwich Arsenal at Plumstead in a friendly on Christmas Day, and Quinn delighted the visiting Scots (including a detachment of the Argyll & Sutherland Highlanders) and impressed the Englishmen with two brilliant goals, one of them a shot from an impossible angle which also had the unfortunate side effect of injuring the goalkeeper's thumb. Then Celtic returned to Scotland, spent a few days at Wemyss Bay and returned to Parkhead to play Airdrie on Hogmanay. This game was won, and Quinn spent the New Year with his family in Croy before returning to Glasgow to play Rangers at Ibrox on New Year's Day. It was as well perhaps for Jimmy, as he toasted the arrival of 1907, that he did not know what an explosive start it was to have for him. 1906 had been tremendous. For a while, 1907 did not look that way at all.

The New Year's Day game was into the second half. The score was 1-1, and the game was even. Although a few rough tackles had gone in, this was nothing more than what normally happened (and still does) in Old Firm games. The referee, the famous Englishman called Mr Kirkham of Burslem near Preston was doing a good job keeping things under control. Joe Hendry, Rangers' left-back, had however been guilty of a few nasty challenges on Celtic's right wing pair of Bennett and McMenemy, and Quinn and he had exchanged words. It was after yet another foul on McMenemy that the incident occurred which had all Scotland arguing well into the 1950s (until such time as the last surviving spectator had died off).

The neutral *Glasgow Herald* states quite blandly that 'he (Mr Kirkham) latterly had to order Quinn off the field. Hendry, who was injured, retired at the same time, but was able to resume'. The Hendry/Rangers version was that Quinn ran across to Hendry, knocked him to the ground and kicked him in the face. The Quinn/Celtic version was that Hendry was already on the ground in his impetus of having brought down McMenemy. Quinn ran across to remonstrate with Hendry, but thought better of it, tried to jump over Hendry but on the damp pitch may have skidded unfortunately into Hendry's face.

Whatever happened, the referee sent Quinn off and Rangers went on to score a winner, ironically through Willie Kivlichan who would later join Celtic. Quinn protested his innocence, but was summoned to appear before the SFA. Celtic then did him no favours by claiming that it was a case of mistaken identity and that it was another unnamed Celt who kicked Hendry in the face. This seemed to contradict, or at least was at variance with Jimmy's original story that he actually attempted to jump over Hendry.

The hearing was on 8 January 1907. Normally a disciplinary hearing would not have taken place at 6 Carlton Place until the end of the month, but there had recently been 'rough play rampant', and Quinn's case was only one of many, albeit the one with the highest profile. Under the chairmanship of Mr J. Liddell of Queen's Park, the committee heard a letter read out from Mr Kirkham. He said that Hendry did indeed foul another Celtic player (Jimmy McMenemy) and he (Kirkham) was about to award a free kick but 'before Hendry could rise, Quinn took a most dangerous jump, his boot coming violently in contact with Hendry's face'. Quinn, to his credit 'went immediately without the slightest demur'.

Even though this now proved that Hendry was *not* knocked down by Quinn, the SFA accepted that Quinn had indeed been guilty of violent conduct. They did not accept Quinn's plea that he 'recollected himself and jumped over the fallen player without to his knowledge touching him'. Quinn was found guilty. A penalty of two months' suspension was proposed while someone else suggested one month; by a vote of 16-6, the longer penalty was imposed.

What actually happened will never of course be discovered now 100 years down the line. Sadly, not even still photographic evidence is available. What must be said in Jimmy's defence, however, was that a deliberate kick in the face does seem to be out of character for a man like Quinn. Quinn, frequently fouled and injured himself, was quite capable of defending his honour, but to knock a man down, then kick him maliciously in the face does not seem to be something that a basically fair-minded man like Quinn would have done. The early twentieth century was indeed a violent time in football circles, but there was code of practice that would not include such thuggery.

If Quinn did do what he was supposed to have done, then he was indeed lucky to get off with two months. *Sine die* would not have been inappropriate. As it was, the newspapers speculated whether Quinn was finished, and certainly it was significant that he was awarded no international honours in 1907, even although his suspension was up by the beginning of March. There did seem to be a certain amount of vindictiveness and spite in the attitude of the establishment.

The name 'Quinn' now split Scottish opinion in two. The pro-Quinn camp, not all of them Celtic supporters, mobilised themselves in an impressive show of loyalty to their fallen and unjustly treated hero. With a certain amount of official backing from the club, notably from director Tom White, a fund was raised to compensate Quinn for loss of earnings during his suspension. Money poured in from the Celtic brake clubs (who had organised a collection among their members), as well as individuals from Scotland, Ireland and the United States, the club directors and his fellow players; a huge sum of over £277 was raised. A concert was held on 6 March 1907 at the St Mungo Halls, at which Jimmy was presented with the sum, a gold watch and a gold pendant for his wife Annie. The proceeds from the concert itself went to charity, and Jimmy promised to make a donation from the amount he had received.

Jimmy accepted the sum of money, but being no orator, did not deliver a fulsome speech. He merely said thanked the crowd, with tears in his eyes, and promised all his devoted fans that they would be paid back on Saturday – this being the day for Quinn's return. It was almost as if it had been meant by Providence. His first game back would be in the Scottish Cup quarter-final, and it was against Rangers at Ibrox!

FIVE

QUINN TRIUMPHANT
1907/08

Quinn's return to play for Celtic at Ibrox on 9 March 1907 may not have quite been the most momentous event in all of Glasgow's rich history hitherto, but everyone acted as if it were. Celtic had, even without Quinn, continued their winning ways, although they had needed three games to get the better of Morton in the Scottish Cup. They were clearly on course for the Scottish League, being well ahead of rivals Dundee and Rangers, and the prospect was beginning to be mooted that Celtic might well become the first team ever to win the Scottish League and the Scottish Cup in the same season. No club had done that before in Scotland (although Preston North End and Aston Villa had done it in England) and Celtic, especially with Quinn now returning, seemed quite capable of achieving the feat.

Serious fears were expressed about Ibrox Park for this game. It was a Scottish Cup quarter-final, and the 'Blue Riband' competition (as the Scottish Cup was then called) often had the ability to draw out more supporters than would normally appear. Rangers were seen as the most likely team to stop Celtic and their supporters would be there in force. But so too would the Celtic support, determined to see the return of the great Jimmy to the scene where he had been so unjustly treated two months previously. Hendry would be playing for Rangers. Unlike Craig in 1905, Hendry had not spoken out in favour of Quinn, and a certain amount of needle was expected between the two of them.

The result of all this was that there would be a massive attendance at Ibrox. Everyone knew that twenty-six people had been killed and hundreds injured there in the Scotland *v*. England game of only five years previously, and apprehension was evident about whether the ground would be able to contain the vast crowd. There was also the precedent of the game on New Year's Day 1905, which had to be abandoned because of crowd encroachment. Curiously, no-one seemed to be worried about the *behaviour* of the supporters, only whether they would be able to fit in safely. Football hooliganism, although not unheard of, was not necessarily yet seen as a major menace in Edwardian Scotland.

The crowd was given as 60,000 (with £1,919 receipts) – a record in British club football at the time – but thousands more climbed walls, rushed turnstiles and were 'lifted over' if they were youngsters. The *Glasgow Herald* tells us 'The crowd was so dense that one of the exit gates was burst open and before order could be maintained, large numbers had gained free admission. In the rush several persons were crushed and had it not been for the admirable service rendered by the mounted police, the disorder might have had more serious consequences.'

It was a cold day for March, with clouds and snow threatening. For Quinn, it was a remarkable experience. He actually had a quiet game, but only because he was always shadowed by three men (Joe Hendry and two others). Taking advantage of this heavy pressure on one man, the rest of the forward line ran riot and the 3-0 scoreline was, if anything, slightly flattering for the Rangers team.

Peter Somers scored within the first ten minutes, and then Quinn was put to the test. On the blind side of the referee, he was kicked by his old enemy Hendry, and then as he lay on the ground a boot was planted, none too gently, on his stomach. This was Quinn's acid test. He might have reacted violently – indeed most men would have – but Quinn rose with dignity and limped away, earning the plaudits of the Press for doing so. He then scored a goal a few minutes later that was mysteriously disallowed, but subsequently had his rewards when Jimmy Hay scored on the point of half-time, and Davie Hamilton soon after the restart.

With Celtic now 3-0 up, Quinn was content to play out time serenely, his point having been proved, laughing to himself at the amateurish attempts of Hendry and others to rile him further with their puerile remarks about Ireland, the Pope, the Fenians and Croy. Frequently, Ibrox was treated to the ludicrous sight of Quinn standing with three defenders while the rest of the Celtic forward line played the ball about to each other.

Quarter of an hour from time, the only threat to Celtic came from the snow which began to fall profusely. Fortunately, the ground was wet and the snow did not lie, although it did impair visibility. At this point, 'the crowd began to skail' (went home or to drier parts), having seen a victory for Celtic that was comprehensive and total, with the added ingredient of justice having been done. Quinn may not have hit the headlines that day, but his mere presence was sufficient to guarantee a victory. Moreover, he had done his reputation no harm at all by his calm reaction to undisguised provocation. It was indeed Quinn's day.

The *Glasgow Herald*, normally no great lover of the Celtic, while sneering at the poor character of the opposition, was reluctantly compelled to admit 'Their [Celtic's] play at Ibrox was a revelation almost touching their early season form when they were indeed an eleven above the average'. Rangers had loads of dash and enthusiasm, but it was the 'methodical precision' of Celtic, particularly the mighty half-back line, which carried the day. The return of Jimmy Quinn had also played a part.

Quinn had a less successful day the following Saturday at Cathkin Park against Third Lanark. He scored, but Celtic went down to only their second League defeat of the season. There were reasons for this reverse in that McNair, Bennett and Somers were all on international duty for Scotland against Ireland at Celtic Park. Quinn was naturally upset at not being with them, but he could not realistically have expected to be chosen when he was only back a week from his suspension. The Wales game had already been played when Quinn was still under suspension, but he still nurtured hopes that he might make it for the England game at Newcastle on 6 April.

The team, when it was announced, amazed everyone. Only two Home Scots were chosen (both from Hearts), and the other nine were Anglo-Scots. The potential controversy over whether Quinn ought to have played or not was overshadowed by the composition of the side and the implication that the Scottish game was not up to very much. Maley was quite upset about this, for he might reasonably have expected four Celts to be in the team. Celtic were reputed to have pondered (not for the first nor last time) the possibility of joining the English League.

It has indeed been a recurring theme throughout Celtic history that Celtic players are not rewarded often enough with Scottish caps. Jimmy McGrory in the 1920s and '30s is the *cause celebre*. Those of the paranoia complex have complained of racial and religious discrimination. Certainly throughout the ages Celtic players, while playing for Scotland, have had to cope with sectarian abuse from some of the crowd who have thought that they had no place in a Scottish line-up, but that is not the same as saying that the selectors have been guilty of religious prejudice.

A more likely explanation lies in the incompetence of those whose job it was to choose the team – normally directors of teams who served a term of a few years as a 'selector'. It all changed once a full-time manager was appointed from the 1960s onwards, although even then a few weird decisions have been made, and not only involving Celtic players.

Whatever Quinn and Celtic may have felt about ill treatment from the Scottish establishment in 1907, there was still a certain amount of unfinished business in the Scottish domestic season as Celtic went for the double of the League and the Scottish Cup in the same season. The League was more or less guaranteed on 23 March when Celtic held Dundee to a 0-0 draw at Parkhead. Dundee had needed to win that game, but Celtic denied them, although the Taysiders were convinced that they had got the ball over the line at one point. The writer of *The Courier*, however, is proud of Dundee's centre half Herbert Dainty. Dainty had a good game and 'kept Jimmie [sic] quiet'. Celtic then beat Queen's Park and the third League Championship in a row was confirmed at Partick Thistle's Meadowside ground on Wednesday 24 April.

The Prince and Princess of Wales (the future King George V and Queen Mary) were in Glasgow that evening (although not at the football), and Rangers were winning back some self respect by beating English Champions Newcastle United 3-0, but it was Celtic at Meadowside who earned all the plaudits. Thistle's goalkeeper Massie defied Celtic for a long time to keep the score at 1-0, but in the closing stages 'he was beaten by Quinn with a shot he never saw', as the *Glasgow Herald* put it.

Celtic had entered the record books, for they were able to bring along with them the Scottish Cup. Curiously, in the latter stages of this competition Quinn seems to have had a quiet time. Perhaps he was out of match practice after such a long enforced lay-off in January and February; perhaps he was depressed about not winning back his Scotland place, and in particular that he had not yet played against England; perhaps he was just being extra careful not to fall foul of referees and the authorities again. Whatever the reason, Quinn did not carry all before him as he had done in the past. He was merely a member of the team… but what a team!

Three games were required to get past Hibs in the semi-final. The first two were depressing 0-0 draws, but then Quinn scored halfway through the first half of the second replay and repeatedly fed Bobby Templeton to do his 'dancing displays' down the left wing. *The Scotsman* then eschews its sympathies for Hibs to tell us that 'the beauty of the movements of the McMenemy, Quinn and Somers trio is unsurpassed in football', as Celtic went on to win 3-0. Much was made in the *Glasgow Herald* of the 'display of temper by all' but passions clearly cooled when the third goal went in.

It was the other Edinburgh team, Hearts, which awaited Celtic in the Scottish Cup final the following week, 20 April 1907. There was a large 50,000 crowd who paid £1,424, in spite of the inclement weather. The Edinburgh men never recovered from the absence through injury of their great defender Charlie Thomson – who was reckoned to be one of the few men in Scotland capable of nullifying the menace of the mighty Quinn. But Hearts did receive some magnanimous treatment from Celtic. Their goalkeeper, Allan, was delayed in traffic jams, and Maley sportingly agreed with referee Mr D. Philp of Dunfermline to await his arrival. It is hard to imagine that happening today!

The first half was goal-less on a bright and breezy spring afternoon, with frequent heavy rainstorms. Hearts had done well to hold Celtic, but the feeling was that once Celtic got ahead, they would not be stopped, given the excellence of Young, Loney and Hay in midfield. This is exactly what happened. Early in the second half, Quinn was charging through and was stopped by McLaren. Curiously enough, Alec McNair in his memoirs claimed that it was he who was fouled, but other sources unanimously say Quinn. The referee blew for a penalty, an award hotly disputed by the Edinburgh men. Willie Orr took the penalty, scored, and then as Hearts began to tire in the face of Celtic's mighty forwards, Peter Somers scored a couple more from service supplied by Alec Bennett, and Celtic won at a canter.

McNair's reminiscences tell us that both of Somers' goals were virtual carbon copies. There was a cross from Bennett to Quinn, then Jimmy stepped over the ball in the first case and left it to Somers, then for Celtic's third goal, Quinn ran in the other direction, taking two men with him, leaving Peter once more in the clear to do the needful. Celtic finished the game well on top.

This defeat marked the collapse of the great Hearts team, a collapse from which they would not recover for fifty years, but it was another great triumph for Celtic and for Quinn. Once again, the man from Croy, without necessarily starring in the game, had been instrumental, by his very presence, in winning a great success for Celtic. Richly had he paid back those who raised the money for him when he was suspended.

The 1906/07 season now fizzled out. Quinn had a penalty saved by a young Port Glasgow goalkeeper called Charlie Shaw; Hearts supporters began their melancholy tradition of bad behaviour whenever Celtic are around by spitting at Celtic fans and players after a cracking 3-3 draw at Tynecastle; and Celtic threw away their opportunity to win all four competitions in the same year when they lost 0-1 to Rangers in the final of the Glasgow Charity Cup.

Bobby Templeton was given the blame for this and never really regained Maley's grace and favour. He overdid the dribbling and showed off in front of the 38,000 crowd when Quinn and others were in the middle waiting for a cross. Rangers, to their credit, and now without Quinn's old foe Joe Hendry, played well enough and regained a certain amount of respect for what had been a shocking season for them and their supporters.

The *Glasgow Herald* was delighted that £1,400 had been raised for charity and paid tribute to the ability of Celtic to 'draw a revenue which is amazing even in these golden days of sporting finance', but then goes on to sneer at the temperament of some of the Celtic players 'who are not at their best when great issues are at stake' – a questionable judgement on the first team to win the 'double'! It was a shame not to win all the trophies, but three out of four was not bad (however much the perfectionist Maley fumed), especially when this includes the Scottish League and the Scottish Cup.

Celtic sailed from Leith at the beginning of June to play four games in Denmark on a short tour. Three were won, one was lost and Quinn was among the goals, but the whole exercise was a light-hearted one. Maley was so shocked at the standard of Danish refereeing that he offered to referee the last two games himself, and Templeton, who had again disgraced himself by selfishly showing off on the left wing, was made to play in the goal! The good people of Copenhagen, however, had a chance to see Celtic, and in particular this man called Quinn.

The following season saw Celtic actually succeed in winning all four trophies, a feat that puts the 1908 side on the same level as that of 1967. Celtic got off to their usual good start, with Quinn's genius never far away from the surface. Indeed, the word 'genius' was used quite freely in the Press of a goal he scored against Airdrie at Parkhead on 21 September to earn Celtic a point in a real roughhouse of a game. There would be repercussions from this match. In the first place because some Celtic fans threw cinders from the terracing – the standard Edwardian manifestation of hooliganism – the club were fined £15 and ordered to post warning notices. Then the referee of the Celtic v. Airdrie game, a Mr J.B. Stark (of Airdrie) was censured for lack of control and was about to begin a suspension of one month, amid general cries that referees and authorities must clamp down on the baddies.

Before his suspension began, Stark was in charge of Celtic again in a game against Hibs at Easter Road and, clearly with a point to prove about how tough he could be, sent off Quinn for charging. Amazingly, Celtic won this shambles of a game 2-1 (Quinn scoring both goals before his dismissal) easily enough though they finished the game with just eight men. Left-back Jamie Weir had been taken off with a broken nose, Quinn was sent off, and Davie Hamilton was sent off for obscene and threatening language – apparently saying to Mr Stark 'I wish I had a f★★★★★★ revolver'.

The *Glasgow Herald* defended Quinn: 'Quinn with that chivalrous desire to personally avenge a fancied wrong to a physically weaker comrade which has previously involved him in trouble charged a Hibernian player in a manner which the referee adjudged merited his dismissal'. It then goes on to say that Quinn was suffering from the rigid enforcement of the 'new order' and that 'many actions more serious by far than Quinn's have brought no penalty'.

Clearly the *Glasgow Herald* is prepared to defend charging. It is also clear that the SFA adjudged Jimmy's dismissal as harsh, for he was merely censured and told to behave, when he might have expected worse given that his previous suspension was for two months. That he might be banned indefinitely was bartered around in Glasgow gossip, but mercy was shown. Hamilton, on the other hand, was given two months, to the delight of the *Glasgow Herald* who said, 'With Quinn we have sympathy; with Hamilton we have none'.

Hamilton's suspension and the continuing feeling that the extroverted Templeton was still *persona non grata* with Maley, meant that Quinn now returned temporarily to the left wing to allow new signing David McLean from Forfar to play in the centre. It was a successful move, with McLean scoring one of the goals in the 2-1 victory that won Celtic the Glasgow Cup for the fourth successive year, albeit at the third attempt on 26 October 1907. It was widely rumoured that Celtic and Rangers had deliberately arranged for the first two games to be draws, ensuring both clubs more money. As it was, the third game raised £1,485, and the grand total was upwards of £3,000. It was easy to be cynical (and this cynicism would have disastrous consequences in the riot in 1909), but the *Glasgow Herald* was at pains to point put the 'honesty' of football. This was, however, a theme that would not go away.

The prolonged suspension of Hamilton and the success of Quinn on the left wing meant that he was allowed to play there for longer than Maley would have liked in ideal circumstances. Quinn himself, although willing to play anywhere he was told – for he was always very loyal and committed – did miss the middle of the park where his bulk and determination were of great benefit to him in the 'rumble them up' thrust of the game at which he excelled. Charging (with the shoulder, not the elbow) was then considered to be part of the game – it was even held to be one of the skills – and Quinn excelled at that. On the left wing, there was more need for speed and ability to cross; Quinn could do that as well, but the centre of the field was where he was at his best.

The team reached New Year with 29 points from 18 games (two points were allowed for a win and one for a draw). Although Celtic were behind the leaders, Falkirk and Dundee, they had games in hand because of their extended Glasgow Cup commitments and could make up the points.

There had been two defeats in the League. One was on the distant field of Pittodrie and the other was at Tynecastle. Celtic tended to do badly at Pittodrie, for it was the only ground on which Celtic's supporters would certainly be in a minority. It was clearly out of reach of the horse-drawn brake clubs who found Motherwell and Kilmarnock no problem. Any supporter who wished to go to Aberdeen would have had to use the train. A few did so, enjoying the company of the players en route, but it was rather expensive for many people to make the trip.

In addition, Aberdeen, alone of all Scottish cities, did not have a large Irish population, so there was no great indigenous Celtic support in Aberdeen. One of the effects, however, of the great Celtic team of the Edwardian era was that support and love for them spread fairly rapidly among the Scottish Protestant population, particularly in areas like Angus, Kincardine and Buchan. Celtic could therefore count upon a small (but by no means overwhelming) support when they played at Aberdeen. Their supporters at north-eastern venues like Aberdeen and

Dundee were genuine football fans who had chosen to follow Celtic, rather than those who had been brought up to it and really, for ethnic and cultural reasons, had little choice.

Celtic's defeat at Pittodrie in September 1907 was a sensation. It had a great effect on the development of football in Aberdeen, where people now believed that their side could compete with the best. For the other defeat, against Hearts in late November, Quinn was on the left wing with Willie Kivlichan in the centre. Kivlichan made absolutely no impact on Charlie Thomson, and it was only when he and Quinn changed places in the latter stages of the game that Celtic looked anything like equalizing.

Then dawned the momentous year of 1908. On New Year's Day, Celtic beat Rangers 2-1 at Parkhead with the immortal forward line of Bennett, McMenemy, Quinn, Somers and Hamilton at full throttle. The 2-1 victory was more emphatic than the scoreline would suggest. Although Quinn did not score, his presence in the centre was significant for both his spraying of passes and the obsession that the Rangers defenders had about him. In particular, Quinn drew left half Jimmy Galt (a robust player who earned and deserved the nickname 'Dirty Galt') away from the more fragile Jimmy McMenemy. While mindful of previous encounters against Rangers when he had been sent off, Quinn nevertheless made sure that whatever Galt dished out, it was paid back in full. It was, however, a far cleaner game than some had been in the recent past between the two sides.

The day after, Quinn, playing with 'rare dash' in the forward line, scored in the 3-0 win over Aberdeen at Parkhead, but late in the game seemed to hurt his toe in an innocent clash with Aberdeen's Alec Halkett. It did not look a serious injury, although Quinn did limp off the field. The toe seemed to pick up an infection a couple of days later and the end result was that Quinn was out until 29 February. Kivlichan proved an able enough deputy, however, and the team kept winning, although Jimmy's toe became the main topic of conversation in Glasgow that winter – even earning a mention in Glasgow's music halls, with the wife complaining that the husband is more interested in Quinn's toe than house and home!

There was a more serious problem with a Celtic player that year. Jimmy Hay, the inspirational captain, was operated on for appendicitis early in the New Year. This was a dangerous procedure in 1908, and it had only been after the operation on King Edward VII (delaying his coronation in 1902) that appendicitis could in any way be treated. Prayers were said at Mass and in private devotions for (the Protestant) Jimmy Hay, and a few, frivolous persons would add a rosary bead or two for Jimmy Quinn's toe.

In fact, Jimmy's toe proved to be a little more serious than was thought, for septicaemia set in and made the patient quite ill. The *Glasgow Herald* was at pains to stress that Quinn had been out 'after a lengthened absence through illness' which it describes as 'troublesome and painful'. The *Herald* is very keen for him however to get fit as quickly as possible for the international match against England was fast approaching and this would surely be Quinn's moment, if he were fit. There was some good news as well, as Quinn's wife Annie had another baby on 2 February – a girl who would be called Annie after her mother. Annie would grow up to be a teacher ('fierce but fair' in the opinion of one of her former pupils) and tenacious in her efforts to keep alive the memory of her illustrious father.

Happily for Celtic, both Hay and Quinn were back in the spring, although in Quinn's case, the rest of his Celtic season was punctuated by international duty and another injury. By 7 March, after a 4-0 win over Hibs, Celtic were clearly in the lead in the League race and Quinn, to the delight of the *Glasgow Herald*, was chosen to go to Dublin to play for Scotland on 14 March. It was, of course, his second trip for he had been there in 1906.

As the party gathered at the Broomielaw on Thursday 12 March, Quinn, nervous as always about travel and still less than totally fit, was apprehensive. Little did he realise that he was about to become the talk of the Emerald Isle with his four goals in Scotland's 5-0 victory. All the goals were good ones and typical of Quinn – a shot from the edge of the box, a 'charge through' and two where he was in the right place at the right time, one following a fine run by R.S. McColl. When the ship left Dublin harbour that night, 'the talk was Quinn, Quinn and more Quinn' and 'never since the days of Charles Stuart Parnell has a man been talked about so much' with Irish newspapers stressing that he was of Irish descent and played for the Glasgow Celtic.

While allowing for a certain amount of Irish hyperbole in such newspaper comments, Quinn could scarcely now be left out for the England game. Indeed, the *Glasgow Herald*, resuming its love affair with Quinn, more or less demands his inclusion, highlighting his 'unselfishness' and 'readiness in making for others' as well as 'utilising himself openings for getting in on goal'. 'Success will in no way spoil his usefulness' it remarked – a comment on the modest demeanour and attitude of the great man.

Before the international happened, however, Quinn had to visit two Scottish cities where the reception was less than friendly. One was to Aberdeen again for the Scottish Cup semi-final. Pittodrie was packed with 20,000 fired-up Northerners and the largest contingent of Celtic fans yet seen at this distant venue. All accounts describe the game as being rough, with both teams perhaps equally to blame for what happened. Quinn kept his cool under intense provocation, however, and it was Celtic through Peter Somers (although some sources say McMenemy) with a late header who won the day and earned a place in the Scottish Cup final. As he left the field, Sunny Jim was pelted with cinders (another example of cinders being the favourite missile of the Edwardian bawheids) and jostled by a few fans. Stones were thrown by the locals at the Celtic charabanc and at the 'cab conveying the referee, Mr Ferguson of Falkirk, breaking a window'.

The Aberdonians were clearly less impressed by Jimmy Quinn than the Dubliners had been the week before, but the *Aberdeen Press & Journal* was at pains to denounce such unacceptable behaviour and blamed it all on the availability of 'cheap ale in the environs of the ground' while wishing for stringent measure to be taken against such 'rascals'. Yet the good relationship between the two teams never weakened. Both managers, Jimmy Philip and Willie Maley, remained friends, and the visit of the Celtic to Aberdeen remained the highlight of the Aberdeen calendar for many years after this unfortunate event.

The following week, Celtic and Quinn took another mauling, this time at the hands of Dundee at Dens Park. The trouble had begun with a soft early penalty being awarded to Dundee. Dean scored with it and, shortly afterwards, Celtic lost the services of Somers and Weir, both injured in horrendous tackles. Quinn received dreadful treatment at the hands of the ludicrously misnamed Herbert Dainty, but once again kept his temper, when a weaker man might have snapped. Yet he could not win the day for an ultimately understrength Celtic. After pressing all second half for the elusive equalizer, it was Dundee who scored an ill-deserved second at the death.

Quinn was determined to avoid trouble as the Scotland *v*. England match was the following week. He and Alec McNair had been selected.

Controversially however, Quinn was on the left wing. There were two reasons for this given out by the selectors, although neither were convincing. One was that Andy Wilson of Sheffield Wednesday was playing so well in the centre that he could not be ignored – indeed he had played well and scored in the trial Home Scots *v.* Anglo Scots on 23 March at Cathkin – and the other was that Scotland needed a burly left winger to 'bump' England's huge right-back, Bob Crompton of Blackburn Rovers. Quinn seemed the man for the job! Celtic fans were less than totally convinced of all this, but at least Jimmy had at last got a place for Scotland against England.

The world's record crowd of over 120,000 on 4 April 1908 (Quinn's inclusion being a factor in persuading such a vast number of people to attend) saw a very competitive game, but they were disappointed in the 1-1 draw. The best moment of football was the run down the left wing by Quinn and the cross for Wilson to put Scotland ahead. England equalized and the second half saw a stalemate as neither team could break through. A little imagination might have put Quinn into the centre, at least as an experiment, to break the deadlock, but this was not forthcoming. The *Glasgow Observer* is disappointed with this, saying that if might have worked for 'at one point it seemed that Scotland's front line was simply Quinn, all Quinn and nothing but Quinn' in the words of a journalist who clearly had a legal background as well as an ability to overstate his case.

The *Glasgow Herald*, consistently pro-Quinn by now, puts it just a little more diplomatically: 'Quinn, alone of all the forwards, could be termed a success. Plucky to a fault, speedy as ever, he in addition showed a resource in a tight corner that amazed most. And it is to be regretted that he did not receive the opportunity to attempt or accomplish more than he did'. This seems to be saying that he should have been in the centre forward position – an opinion held universally after the match among the 120,000 spectators.

If Jimmy and the rest of Scotland were disappointed with the England match (although it did bring a share in the British International Championship) joy would soon be forthcoming on the Celtic front. April 1908 saw Celtic lift the two Scottish trophies for the second year in a row.

A routine defeat of Queen's Park at Hampden in the League on 11 April was followed by the Scottish Cup final on 18 April. This meant that Quinn played at Hampden on three Saturdays in a row, and scored on two of them. Jokes went around that Hampden should be called 'Quinnden' or that it was Jimmy's home from home, and that the train from Croy should be redirected round the ground.

The Scottish Cup final was a mismatch as Celtic put St Mirren to the sword to the tune of 5-1 and visibly eased up towards the end lest they humiliate the Paisley men. The weather was beautiful 'because God wanted to see Jimmy Quinn' as a Glasgow comedian put it. Quinn predictably scored his goal, (although St Mirren were convinced that it was 'fisted through' to him) but he was modest enough to admit that Alec Bennett's two goals were better than his, and he remained full of praise for that master technician Jimmy McMenemy. It was, however, a virtuoso team performance and the newspapers enthused about 'delightful forward play' and that Edwardian cliché 'intricacy of movement'.

The legend of the great team was enhanced. Indeed, this was its apogee. A man going in to a bar and wishing to buy three halves of whisky would say 'Young, Loney and Hay' (because they were three 'halfs' of the best) and a grandfather playing with his baby granddaughter's fingers would not say 'This little piggie went to market…' but it would be 'Bennett, McMenemy, Quinn, Somers and Hamilton…' – and the greatest of these was Quinn.

There remained the League to be won. Celtic celebrated their Scottish Cup victory by thrashing a woefully under-strength Hearts side 6-0 on the Holiday Monday 20 April, with Quinn 'tearing past defenders as if they didn't exist' and scoring a great hat-trick. This meant that Celtic could win the title at Ibrox Park on Saturday 25 April. This day would also be Maley's fortieth birthday, and the players were determined to give him a great present.

They did so in fine April sunshine, but the manner of the victory, while showing Celtic to great credit, was a disgrace to Rangers and embarrassed Scottish football. Following due respect for ex-Prime Minister Sir Henry Campbell-Bannerman (a Glaswegian) who had died a few days previously, the game began ominously when Quinn was chopped down in the first minute. The referee, Mr Faichnie of Falkirk, had a terrible job and was much sympathised with in the Press. Once again, Quinn was targeted by the brutal half-back line of May, Taylor and Galt, and after twenty-five minutes he was carried off with injuries to both thighs as the villains smirked and the crowd bayed. He had hoped to come back at half-time, but could hardly move. He thus winced as McNair and Hamilton received similar treatment, but smiled when the full-time whistle indicated that Alec Bennett's goal was enough to win the match and the Championship for Celtic.

Rangers' humiliation was complete when Quinn hobbled towards them at the end. They might have expected a mouthful of abuse, or even a triumphalist cry, but there was no need for such insecurity. Quinn merely shook their hands, thus winning a great victory over them as a human being in addition to what he and his team had achieved on the park. Twice in recent years, Rangers had succeeded in getting Quinn sent off. They had tried the same on this day, but Quinn did not rise to it. He did not need to. So they had crocked him instead, but Quinn was still happy. His team had now won the Scottish League for four years in a row, and he had been a glorious part of it.

There still remained the Glasgow Charity Cup to complete the quadruple. Quinn's injuries sustained at the hands of the Rangers thugs on 25 April were severe ones and he did not play in the remaining fixtures of the season, until the Charity Cup final on 30 May. In view of the perceived bad blood between Celtic and Rangers, it was perhaps as well that Rangers were avoided and that Quinn's teammates were able to deal with Partick Thistle and Clyde. It was also as well that Queen's Park, having amazed even their own supporters by beating Rangers, had to delay the Charity Cup final until the end of May because of a pre-arranged tour of Denmark. This allowed Jimmy time to recover.

Recover he did, and scored the middle goal of three (McMenemy notching the other two) as Celtic beat Queen's Park 3-0 at Hampden. The Lord Provost was there in brilliant sunshine and although the game was 'on the forceful side with several nasty incidents taking place' Celtic were now able to enter football immortality and to be talked about in the same reverential terms as they now talk about Jock Stein's team in 1967. What Jock Stein did in 1967 was introduce an element of uncertainty about which was the best Celtic team of all time... before 1967, there had been little doubt.

As Quinn wandered about Croy that summer (he seldom strayed far from home) he must have wondered how long he could continue, given the extent of his injuries. But he was not quite thirty, and felt that there was power there yet. He wanted to go on. He loved Celtic, loved Maley and loved the Celtic crowd. He loved football, and still had a desire to win a game for Scotland against England.

He must however, have entertained some misgivings about how he would get on next season with his old friend Alec Bennett. Bennett, after several glorious years for Celtic, had at last accepted the money that had been offered him time and time again to sign for Rangers. Jimmy was sad about this, and wondered whether religion might have been a factor (Bennett was not a Catholic). Jimmy would have hoped that this wasn't the case. His wife was not a Roman Catholic originally, and for this reason he hated bigotry. It would sadden him every July to see the visible rise in tension in nearby Kilsyth as the festival of hate was being prepared and his local hotheads in Croy prepared to defend themselves at Finger Post Corner if necessary. They were clearly those on both sides who would have welcomed the fight, but Jimmy deplored this, for it was surely alien to Scotland.

Jimmy remained convinced that the best way to ensure treatment and respect for his religion and for his parents' nationality was to infiltrate, as it were, and become part of Scottish society, while welcoming those of other religions (and of none) into the Celtic team. It was a subject that was seldom mentioned in the dressing room, yet Quinn knew that his friend and rival Davie McLean (a Scottish Presbyterian who was content to call himself an atheist) wasn't always happy about the overtly Catholic atmosphere at the club, and in particular the omnipresent RC clergymen with their benevolent but persistent appeals for help in worthwhile causes.

Quinn would have hated to think that people would be deterred from Celtic because of all this. He was himself a regular attendee at Mass and at Confession, but accepted that other people were brought up in other ways. He was not so arrogant as to think that his was the only possible way, and he recalled the much-quoted dictum of Willie Maley that 'it is not a man's creed or his nationality that counts; it's the man himself'. Maley knew a thing or two... after all, he had just created the greatest team on earth and he, Jimmy Quinn, was proud to be part of it.

SIX

QUINN THE HERO
1908-1910

Following the phenomenal season of 1907/08, it was hardly surprising that 1908/09 was, in comparative terms, a failure. It was a curious season. The team did, however, manage to win the Championship in odd circumstances at the end of the season, following the even stranger happenings resulting from their inability to win the Scottish Cup for the third year in a row. The Glasgow Cup was another bizarre phenomenon, with one performance in particular that does not allow for rational explanation.

For Quinn personally, it was another great season, and this time comparatively injury free. He scored 29 goals for Celtic (a total that he had bettered only once when he scored 30 in 1906/07) and he earned himself a trip to the Crystal Palace to play for Scotland against England. Once again, the name 'Quinn' was never far away from the lips of Scotsmen when football was discussed.

Celtic would struggle through the loss of Alec Bennett. Rangers had at last persuaded Alec to join them. Alec never played as well for Rangers as he did in his glory days for Celtic and indeed must, one feels, often have questioned whether he did the right thing in crossing the city. At Parkhead he had been part of a wonderful outfit with great players and great companions. At Ibrox, although success would come as William Wilton painstakingly built up a good side, it would not be as immediate or as spectacular as that of Celtic. In later years, Alec would apparently confess that he had been a fool to leave Parkhead.

To fill the right wing position, Celtic would try Dan Munro and occasionally Willie Kivlichan (who had done the opposite from Bennett and joined Celtic from Rangers), but the fluency was never quite achieved and Quinn did not always receive as much service as he had enjoyed in previous seasons. This did not prevent him from scoring, but it meant that often he had to forage as well as finish.

The season started at Cappielow, with Quinn scoring four goals and 'performing outstanding individual play'. He then scored in the next game against Kilmarnock, but once again got himself injured at Dens Park in a 1-2 defeat on 29 August 1908. Celtic were denied a stonewall penalty by referee Mr Robertson of Queen's Park – a man with whom they had seldom had happy relations following his sending off of Jimmy Quinn in 1905. More importantly, perhaps, Quinn's injury resulted in Jimmy missing virtually all of September.

The Glasgow Cup in the autumn of 1908 was a funny business. In Quinn's absence, Celtic had been taken to a replay by Queen's Park before winning through. Then the same thing happened against Rangers, something that did little to douse speculation that all this was happening for financial reasons as gates of 45,000 to 50,000 would invariably appear for first games and replays. Even sober newspapers like the *Glasgow Herald* and *The Scotsman* were not above raising their eyebrows at this, with the *Herald* in particular waxing lyrical about the disruption caused to Scottish League fixtures by the Glasgow FA's insistence on using Saturdays, even for their replays. The Glasgow FA were, of course, older than the Scottish League and could therefore apparently claim precedence… and of course with the prospect of 50,000 crowds, money talked rather loudly.

Quinn was barely fit for the first Rangers game on 26 September 1908, but there was little doubt about his fitness a week later. Everyone was impressed by the brilliant goal he scored on 3 October in the Ibrox replay of the Glasgow Cup semi-final. Quinn picked up the ball just inside the Rangers' half following a crafty one-two with Alec McNair, charged through four men, then hammered home a scorcher from the edge of the penalty box to put Celtic into the final against Third Lanark.

Third Lanark were not expected to give Celtic much bother, but played above themselves to earn a replay after Quinn had put Celtic ahead. Yet for so long in the second half, Thirds were indebted to the brilliant play of goalkeeper Jimmy Brownlie.

The game had been played on 17 October in front of 40,000 fans, and the *Glasgow Herald* had the temerity to indirectly countenance the possibility that something underhand was going on. The leader writer does this by saying that he has little sympathy with the conspiracy theorists and states

QUINN THE HERO 1908-1910

that '...the arranged draw in Association football is practically an impossibility viewed from any aspect'. The very fact that this idea is mentioned in the middle-class *Herald* at all shows that it has been seriously discussed beyond the terraces and the paper is clearly employing a device (beloved of the Latin author Cicero) called *praeteritio* – where one apparently denies something, but in so doing, does in fact draw it to everyone's attention!

A certain disillusionment of the fans could be seen perhaps the following Saturday, when the second game of the Glasgow Cup final was played. This time the score was 2-2 and Quinn was unfortunate in that he hit the post and had several other 'dashes and tries'. Only 25,000 appeared at Hampden on Saturday 24 October for this encounter, with rumours sweeping Glasgow that the game would be yet another draw – rumours that turned out to be correct. There would, of course, six months later, be drastic consequences of all this drawing of games in which a replay with a big crowd was a possibility – or should one say, an incentive?

The third game was played on the following Wednesday afternoon in front of a far smaller crowd of 18,000. This time there was a positive result, but it was an incredible 4-0 win for Third Lanark! This brought to an end a fine run from Celtic in the Glasgow Cup (a much-treasured tournament then and one that they had won for the past four years) and it was a very difficult result for Edwardian Scotland to analyse. In terms of a shock, it can possibly be paralleled in subsequent history by Celtic's defeat by Partick Thistle in the League Cup final of 1971 or by the defeats in the early years of the twenty-first century by Inverness Caledonian Thistle. Phrases like 'debacle' 'rout' and 'humiliation akin to that of Napoleon nigh on 100 years ago at Moscow' were used in the Press.

Little excuse seems possible. Jamie Weir, the left-back, was out for Celtic and the team was handicapped by a bad injury to influential winger Davie Hamilton early in the first half, but this does not really explain the sad lack of fight by a team who were still considered, and quite rightly, to be the best team in the world. Players' memoirs and Maley's own reminiscences eschew the memory of this dreadful afternoon. The most commonly touted explanation was that the Celtic players were making a point to Maley and the rest of the Celtic establishment that they were unhappy at not being given a bonus for their part in achieving two draws and earning the club even more money.

Teams who are in dispute with their management seldom play well. A similar mood of disillusionment was picked up by the fans, for Celtic's first two games in November 1908 (against Partick Thistle and Port Glasgow), both at Parkhead, were watched by minuscule crowds of less than 5,000 – a phenomenon not entirely to be explained away by bad weather or mediocre opposition. The point having apparently been made by both players and fans, the team then rallied and with Quinn back on song and McMenemy in splendid form, Celtic did not lose another game until Boxing Day on a snow-covered pitch against Clyde.

Indeed, the form in the last two months of 1908 was splendid. Quinn scored two fine goals against Airdrie on 21 November, one a great header from a corner, the other a 'great long shot off the post after he burst through'. On 12 December, as Celtic beat Hibs 2-0 at Parkhead, Quinn scored in a lovely move with Jimmy McMenemy and he 'was head and shoulders the best of the twenty-two, his skill and dash recalling his best days'. Then, on 19 December, Celtic registered their first ever League victory at Pittodrie, Quinn's 'brilliant and chivalrous play' doing much to win over Aberdonians and to build bridges after the ill feeling of the previous March.

The calendar year of 1908 was thus brought to a close with Quinn in excellent form. In fact one of his rivals for scoring was none other than centre half Willie Loney. It was of course common practice for teams to employ attacking centre halves in that era, and Celtic played that game to perfection – the difference between Celtic and the rest being that Quinn was always mobile enough to change places with Loney when Loney went forward. In this respect one can perhaps detect a similarity between Quinn and Chris Sutton of 100 years later in that Sutton can, when necessary, defend as well as attack. John Charles of Leeds United, Juventus and Wales in the 1950s could also behave in such a way.

The *Glasgow Herald* never failed to laud Quinn. It congratulated Maley and the rest of the Celtic management team for rearing its own side, for bringing them to fruition and for showing the rest of Scotland what an entertaining game football could be. Quinn was singled out, but Jimmy would have been embarrassed at all this, for he himself never lost any opportunity to sing the praises of his two inside forwards, Jimmy McMenemy and Peter Somers. There was also of course the mighty halfback line of Young, Loney and Hay, still in its prime.

1909 dawned with a fine 3-1 win at Ibrox, but thereafter form was not as impressive as it had been over the past four seasons. There were reasons for this in that Bennett was sorely missed and, after the middle of March,

Willie Loney was also sidelined for the rest of the season. Credit must also be paid to one or two other teams in the League, Dundee in particular, who mounted a real challenge to Celtic and would have cause to be aggrieved at the way in which the League was eventually decided.

Quinn continued to dominate the talk of the nation. He kept a lower profile than of late, concentrating more on the job of leading the line (i.e. receiving the ball in the centre of the field and distributing). He scored fewer goals in the early part of the year, although he did manage a hat-trick when Celtic played a rare visit to Logie Green in Edinburgh to play Leith Athletic in the Scottish Cup, the middle goal being a twenty-yard scorcher. On 24 February in a lacklustre win over Aberdeen at Parkhead 'Quinn's shooting and individual work were the only source of trouble to the Northerners'.

Celtic were well behind in their League fixtures thanks to the delays caused by the Glasgow Cup. They suffered a significant defeat at home to Rangers in mid-March when they lost 2-3 in a dirty, unpleasant game. Quinn scored the second goal in the last minute when he chested a ball over the line, but he had been injured again and looked out of sorts. He was similarly stale the following week when Clyde and Celtic played a dull, goal-less draw in the Scottish Cup semi-final.

He made up for it in the replay, however, as he and Somers scored the goals that put Celtic into their third consecutive Scottish Cup final. Once again Quinn's admirers in the *Glasgow Herald* office went into overdrive: 'The tie will live for one item and that was Quinn's goal. The centre has done wonderful things in his career but it is questionable if he ever added to his known dash such fine football qualities as he exhibited in the taking of the first goal of the match. In a zig-zag run he outwitted four or five opponents, controlling the ball with nice exactitude and wound up not with the usual wild drive but with a judiciously placed shot far out of the goalkeeper's reach'.

On the international scene, Jimmy played in the Scottish League team which beat the English League 3-1 at Celtic Park on 27 February 1909. The *Glasgow Herald* was ecstatic about how Quinn and Harold Paul of Queen's Park played with 'an electric flash'. Paul scored the first goal after a fine interchange with Quinn, and then Quinn headed a glorious second after a Paul cross. The third was a Quinn header from a Bennett cross. Unfortunately, Quinn sustained a slight leg injury, compelling his withdrawal from the game against Wales on the Monday.

Both he and Paul, however, were chosen however for the England game, this time at Crystal Palace on 3 April. The team was given an ecstatic send-off from Glasgow Central Station on the Friday morning. It says a great deal for Scotland's love of football and of their team that there was a similar crowd there on the Sunday night to welcome them back, even after a depressing 0-2 defeat.

It seems to have been an unlucky game for both Quinn and Scotland, and it might have been better if Peter Somers had been chosen to play alongside him rather than the ineffective George Wilson of Newcastle United. England went two up in the early part of the game, and then Scotland pressed throughout the second half. Quinn had a shot from the edge of the penalty box that went just wide, then he rose to a brilliant header that came off the bar with the goalkeeper beaten. To crown it all, Scotland missed a penalty. Jimmy was upset at all this, for he wanted so much (as did the entire nation) to beat England in the most important game of the year.

The drama of April 1909 was just about to begin, however. It centred on the Celtic *v.* Rangers Scottish Cup final on 10 April at Hampden. Quinn, of course, remembered the 1904 Cup Final when he had scored the famous hat-trick that propelled him to stardom. When he scored the first goal of the game in 1909, he might have felt that the same was about to happen again. It was a fine goal too, which he headed after 'a lofty punt' and he was twice 'knocked off his balance' as he went for it. It was a goal 'possible only to Quinn', in the opinion of *The Scotsman* reporter. The goal left Celtic one-up at half-time.

But Rangers now had Alec Bennett, and crucially played him in the centre of the field where Celtic were without the great Willie Loney. Joe Dodds, a natural attacking left-back and comparatively inexperienced at this stage of his career, gradually lost out to Bennett and within the last fifteen minutes Rangers scored twice. A Rangers victory now seemed likely, but with time running out, their goalkeeper Rennie fumbled a mishit shot from Dan Munro and stepped over the line with the ball in his hands as he tried to avoid a shoulder charge from Jimmy Quinn. Celtic had equalized. Another draw in a cup game; another big gate; another raising of eyebrows by a cynical public

Matters were not helped by the obviously cordial relationship between the two teams (at least at managerial level), suggesting all sorts of cosy deals. Maley on the Tuesday suggested that there should be extra time or play to a finish in the replay on Saturday 17 April. He had cause for not wanting yet another replay, for Celtic now had eight League games to play before the end of April, when the season was to end. Yet another match would have more or less compelled Celtic to play a game a day.

In the event, there was no third game but the circumstances were far from what anyone would have wanted. In spite of all the talk about fixes, another 60,000 appeared at Hampden on Saturday 17 April. This time Rangers scored first through Gordon and for a long time looked on top, but then Jimmy Quinn came yet again to Celtic's rescue halfway through the second half with a goal following a well-placed corner kick. After that, both teams came close but clearly tired towards the end.

In fact both teams had good reason for being tired, given the sheer amount of games that they had played that season, but the crowd put a worse interpretation on this. They felt that both teams had eased off and settled yet for another replay. What did not help was an uncertainty among several players that there might be extra time, and Celtic's men in particular hung around after the final whistle blew. But Mr Stark of Airdrie shook hands with everyone in sight, picked up the ball and walked off.

A few hotheads crossed the barrier. The police, of course, were in strength outside the ground to supervise the departure of spectators. More and more people came on the field, some of them perhaps anxious to shake hands with Jimmy Quinn or some other hero, and then a few cinders from the track round the pitch were thrown, in fun more than anything else. As frequently happens, trouble starts suddenly and irrationally and no-one can point the finger at anyone in particular. Within minutes crush barriers were broken, goalposts next, fires lit and Hampden had a full scale and very serious riot on its hands.

Mercifully no-one was killed and such injuries as were sustained were slight ones, but Hampden was devastated, and there was 'ungovernable savagery' on view as policemen were beaten up, and policeman and firemen were pelted with stones and cinders. At one point, amazingly, the police actually threw stones at the mob in order to protect the firemen trying to put out the blaze in the pavilion. Scottish football and Scottish society in general indulged itself in one of its periods of navel-gazing, but in fact no lasting harm was done other than that it was made plain to clubs the dangers of taking fans for granted. Yet it did not work entirely, for the next two Scottish Cup finals of 1910 and 1911 both went to replays...

The players were never in any direct danger, and in any case escaped, although it must have been a terrifying moment for them. Alec Maley, the brother of Celtic's manager, rescued the Scottish Cup from the mob, and no-one was killed or seriously injured. There was also not the slightest hint of any sectarian violence, although a few subsequent histories have tried to play to the gallery by implying this. It did, however, show the authorities that in a society where there is gross poverty and ignorance, there is often a very fine line between civilization and anarchy. The riot died down as quickly as it had started, and by about seven o'clock that night, Glasgow's South Side was calm, even though Scotland's showpiece stadium was destroyed and would remain out of action for some considerable time.

It was also perhaps the forerunner of things to come in that the stability of Victorian society had broken down. There was an increasingly strong Labour Party and women were demanding the vote. It seemed that everyone was asserting themselves, and that there was a certain amount of anger around. Some anger was justified at things like poverty and poor housing. This violent behaviour was certainly not defensible, but it did show, perhaps, that none-too-bright young men were increasingly needing an outlet for violent urges.

Very soon, Celtic had other things to bother them, for on the very night (Monday 19 April) that the SFA decided that there would be no repeat performance and that the Scottish Cup for 1909 was to be withheld, Celtic were beginning their quest to win the League. They had played 26 games and had 39 points. Dundee had 48 points from 33 games. Two points were allowed for a win in 1909, so it followed that if Dundee won their last game on 24 April against Queen's Park, they would have 50 points. Celtic therefore needed 12 points from 8 games – or four wins and four draws – but all games, the Scottish League decreed with no apparent flexibility, had to be played by the end of April: 12 points were therefore required in twelve days.

Even allowing for Celtic's tight schedule, Dundee's two newspapers *The Courier* and *The Advertiser* were united in their outrage that Celtic knew exactly what they had to do, whereas Dundee could only sit and wait. The fixture chaos had been brought about by Celtic's prolonged involvement in the Glasgow Cup in October with its many replays. Two Saturdays had been used up by the Scottish Cup final. There had also been an apparently arrogant refusal to play games off in midweek on winter afternoons when attendances would have been minimal. Dundee were thus disadvantaged. In addition, more tellingly, *The Courier* pointed out that 'Celtic have Quinn, and Jimmie can do an awful lot'.

Celtic thus played on Monday, Wednesday, Thursday, Saturday, Monday, Wednesday, Thursday, Friday. Quinn played in all eight games. Hardly surprisingly, he did not score in every game – indeed he even missed a penalty in the draw at Hamilton Accies on the first Wednesday – but he scored hat-tricks against Motherwell on Monday 26 April and Queen's Park on Wednesday 28 April.

In this run in, Celtic inevitably sustained injuries and suffered from exhaustion, but were greatly indebted to fringe players like David McLean and Willie Kivlichan, even borrowing an amateur from Hamilton Accies called John Atkinson, who thus played against Celtic one day and for them the next – and scored twice! He would subsequently disappear into oblivion, but could boast of playing alongside the mighty Jimmy Quinn.

Dundee had indeed won their only remaining game against Queen's Park on 24 April, and had thus reached 50 points. This game, of course, had to be played at Cathkin Park, for Hampden was out of commission and Cathkin was also the venue for Celtic's appearance on 28 April, where Quinn scored his sixth goal in forty-eight hours. The Queen's Park side were under-strength, but the Celtic team were described in strange Edwardian prose as a 'kittenish eleven' – such was the commitment, fitness and wholehearted loyalty of the players.

By this time, excitement was at fever pitch and the question was whether Celtic could stand this test of endurance. In fact the same eleven men took the field on three successive nights for three away fixtures. After the Queen's Park game, Celtic travelled to Edinburgh on the Thursday, where they could have won the League but lost an early goal and simply lacked the physical strength to come back at a fiercely determined Hibs side who did not want to see them win the title on their patch.

It thus all depended on the last fixture at Hamilton on the beautiful evening of 30 April. Superhuman strength was required, but at time like these, one relies on the superbly great, like Jimmy Quinn. Once again concentrating on his role of leading the line and feeding players as well as charging through and scoring, Jimmy was a tower of strength. He fed Davie Hamilton for the first goal, hit the bar with a header but then sustained an injury and had to play on the right wing. This was no real problem, however, for it allowed Davie McLean to come into the centre. Even as a passenger on the wing, Quinn had two men on him and this allowed Jimmy

McMenemy space to score the second goal in the second half. Celtic now seemed secure but they still had to sweat when Hamilton Accies scored towards the end. Now the versatile Quinn had to defend, but he gritted his teeth, ignored his injury and helped Sunny Jim, Joe Dodds and Jimmy Hay boot everything up the field until the blessed sound of the referee's whistle brought Celtic their fifth successive League title.

All of Scotland was impressed by this feat of endurance, even the Dundee papers who conceded that this was a great Celtic side and that 'in Quinn, all things are possible'. In fact the injury that he sustained at Douglas Park that night finished his season, and he took no part in the Glasgow Charity Cup. Possibly as a result of Jimmy's absence, Celtic lost this tournament to Rangers. Thus there were now a few signs of mortality beginning to appear on Maley's great side. Bennett had been gone for a season and had been much missed, and others would soon depart as well, but Quinn was still there. And Quinn, no matter how battered and bruised, always felt that he had points to prove.

Jimmy had been awarded a benefit match at the start of the 1909/10 season. It was a light-hearted affair between Celtic and Rangers, in which Celtic beat Rangers 8-4 in a game that lasted thirty-five minutes each half, in which teams were allowed to substitute and there seemed to be a conspiracy to allow everyone else except Quinn to score. He was nevertheless cheered to the echo by his 8,000 fans and applauded by Rangers' players and supporters, clearly prepared to let bygones be bygones.

A further attempt to play down any rivalry between the teams came when both provided players for a Select XI against the Rest of Glasgow at the ground of West of Scotland Cricket club, Hamilton Crescent. This ground had, of course, been the venue of the world's first ever international football match between Scotland and England in November 1872. Quinn scored a hat-trick as the Celtic/Rangers composite side won 5-1.

More serious stuff came in the Glasgow Cup. After a tactless draw with Queen's Park (made all the more sinister by the fact that both goals were obvious goalkeeping mistakes), Celtic and Quinn were rampant in the replay, in which Queen's Park 'collapsed in the second moiety' as Quinn scored a hat-trick. This was on Wednesday 6 October 1909 and the final against Rangers was played at a partially restored Hampden on Saturday 9 October.

The authorities must have been praying that this game would not be drawn, but in the event there was only one goal in it, and it was scored in spectacular fashion by Jimmy Quinn. It was of a kind of which reports stated 'only he is capable' and it came from a mishit clearance by Rangers left-back McKenzie. The ball skied into the air and four men charged for it – three Rangers (namely McKenzie himself, right-back Law, goalkeeper Herbert Lock) and Jimmy Quinn. Quinn, although limping from a light knock, was there first as all four collided at the edge of the box, the ball ended up in the back of the net and Quinn finished up with three Rangers on top of him in a manner akin to the collapse of a ruck in rugby. Reputedly, two of the Rangers players said 'Well done, Jimmy' but the third was a little less charitable as Quinn disentangled himself.

This was his Quinn's fifth Glasgow Cup medal, and before the month of October was out, Celtic had re-established themselves at the top of the Scottish League and Quinn himself had played in another representative match. This was for the Scottish League against the Irish League at Firhill. The Scotsmen won 2-0, Quinn scoring one from a Willie Kivlichan cross, then himself crossing for Sandy McFarlane of Dundee to score the other.

Celtic continued into the winter, still winning games, albeit a little less convincingly than in previous seasons, but Quinn reserved his best goal for Christmas Day at Rugby Park, Kilmarnock. December had been a bad month, but the frost had thawed, leaving Rugby Park a veritable mud heap. Such conditions suited Jimmy and the goal he scored that day (the only goal of the game, just before half-time) has been described as his best ever. Celtic had been struggling without Eck McNair and had a few defenders less than totally fit. Quinn had been back helping out his rearguard. The ball suddenly came to him about ten yards within his own half. His marker, Barrie, slipped in the mud and Jimmy realised that his route to goal was clear. No point in passing because the ball might stick in the mud, so Jimmy, head down, charged forward with four or five Kilmarnock defenders several yards behind him. At twenty-five yards from goal and fearing that at least one of them was catching him up, Jimmy shot a pile-driver that gave goalkeeper Aitken no chance. The 10,000 fans, Killie and Celtic alike, erupted at such brilliance, and although Christmas in 1909 in Scotland was nothing like the festival that it would become later on in the century, people would still talk about Quinn's Christmas goal. A Scottish soldier at Passchendaele, for example, in 1917 would describe the conditions as 'It's like Kilmarnock on Quinn's Christmas'.

The New Year's Day game of 1910 between Celtic and Rangers at Parkhead was in the tradition of Old Firm (as they were now being called) games. It was tough and bruising with heavy casualties on both sides as a 1-1 draw was played out. It was Davie Hamilton who scored Celtic's goal, but Quinn once again was the decoy man who drew more than one Rangers defender to him and accepted the inevitable punishment that was to be dished out. Yet he kept 'a calm seugh' and the 1-1 draw was a good result from Celtic. Fifteen days later, another Jimmy Quinn entered the world when Annie Quinn gave birth to their fifth child.

From New Year until mid-April, Celtic lost only once and that was on a snowy day at Love Street on 29 January when a wiser referee would have decreed that no football was possible. The 12,000 crowd pelted the players and officials with snowballs throughout the game, and invaded the field (briefly) as Sunny Jim Young was sent off. Quinn had scored early that day, but it was St Mirren who lowered the colours of the Celts.

Apart from that reverse, Celtic, with Quinn in consistently good form, beat everyone that came their way. He scored in most games, notably a hat-trick against Third Lanark in the Scottish Cup on 12 February (a dash down the left wing, a hard shot and a prod home, although injured) and against Partick Thistle in the League on 26 March. On 19 February, when Celtic were visited by Aberdeen at Parkhead on Scottish Cup business, he triggered off some bizarre behaviour among Aberdeen fans.

McMenemy had opened the scoring and then when Quinn scored a second goal midway through the second half, the douce Aberdonians (about 200 of them apparently, and clearly enjoying a rare trip to Glasgow) started to sing 'Auld Lang Syne'! It is difficult to work out the context of this strange happening. It will be remembered that when Celtic came to Aberdeen in 1908, there had been trouble. Since then, however, bridges had been built, but why should Aberdeen fans get sentimental about Jimmy's second goal? Was it sarcasm and aimed at their own inept team's inability to win at Parkhead? Or was it appreciation of the great Quinn, who was after all the hero of all Scotland and would soon become more so? Or perhaps it was simply some drunken attempt by good-natured Aberdonians far from home to cheer up what was a poor performance on a cold, miserable day!

Celtic received a severe check to their aspirations on 12 March 1910 when they lost their Scottish Cup semi-final to neighbours Clyde at Shawfield. In Quinn's case, it was an even more personal sense of 'neighbour', for his direct opponent that day was Tommy McAteer – who not only came from Croy, but actually lived in Smithston Row! There could even have been yet another Croy man in that semi-final, for Maley toyed with the idea of playing Philip Quinn (Jimmy's brother, who would later go on to play for Hamilton Accies) in the goal for Celtic, but opted instead for Welsh international Leigh Roose, whom he had picked up on loan from Sunderland.

It was a sad mistake. The eccentric Roose showed off and failed to demonstrate the necessary concentration for the job, even running out to shake the hand of a Clyde man after he scored! The Celtic team was weakened by injury and suspension and Tommy McAteer was able to prevent Quinn from scoring. Quinn did, however, lay off to Kivlichan for Celtic's only goal and should have scored himself before Chalmers scored Clyde's third in their 3-1 victory. It was Celtic's first defeat in a Scottish Cup tie since going down to Hearts in 1906. Thus did Clyde reach their first ever Scottish Cup final. Tommy McAteer did not win the Scottish Cup that year for Clyde, because Dundee would beat them (at the third attempt), but he joined Celtic immediately afterwards where he would have more success in the 1911 Scottish Cup.

Celtic persevered in the League, and won it with some comfort. Ironically, Quinn was out injured on the day that the title was won on Monday 25 April 1910. The League could have been won on Saturday 23 April, when Celtic visited their closest challengers Falkirk, but Celtic lost this game 0-2. Quinn received a severe mauling from some coarse defenders and limped off in the fifty-second minute, effectively ending his season prematurely. He thus watched as Celtic drew 0-0 with Hibs on the Monday in front of a scant crowd to win their sixth Championship in a row; he was also still a spectator as they exited the Glasgow Charity Cup to Third Lanark on 2 May.

So 1910 was another good year for Quinn as far as Celtic was concerned, but it was also the only year that Quinn played for Scotland in all three home internationals. On 26 February at Blackburn, Quinn played for the Scottish League against the English League in a 3-2 win. On that same day, his brother Philip played one of his two friendly games for Celtic – in goal in a friendly at Falkirk. Celtic would lose this game, but the *Kirkintilloch Gazette* is proud of Philip, saying that he 'keeps a clever goal' and goes on to imply that he had played for them in the goal before. It then reminds everyone that he 'once toured with Celtic as a back'. Sadly, Philip never played an official, competitive game for Celtic.

Big brother Jimmy played well enough at Blackburn. He scored the second goal 'from an acute angle giving the surprised goalkeeper no chance' and his general play earned this tribute from his ever-admiring reporter at the *Glasgow Herald*:'Quinn played more football than even his fondest admirers give him credit for. He was the usual dashing forward, bustling the backs and thereby giving others chances but he developed an intricacy of movement that rendered him in consequence more to be feared than ever'.

It was thus no surprise to find him in the team to play Wales at Kilmarnock on 5 March. Scotland scored the only goal of the game through Andrew Devine of Falkirk, but it was an unimpressive match. The *Glasgow Herald*, however, says: 'Quinn alone of the forwards pleased. Peake never left his side, but it takes more than a Peake to hold Quinn, and his dash and enthusiasm, better supported, would have brought more convincing results'.

On 19 March, Scotland lost to Ireland in Belfast. This rare event, only the second defeat to Ireland since 1884, was much mourned in Scotland and cannot entirely be explained away by the absence through injury of Jimmy McMenemy. The *Glasgow Herald* has this cryptic and cynical comment to make about Quinn: 'Quinn was shadowed by McConnell, sometimes unscrupulously. If such methods are to be always in operation, Scotland must perforce look for a centre of less fame'. It would appear then that Quinn was a victim of his own success in that, such was his renown, he was not allowed to play his own game! Quinn of course had experienced this all his career.

Jimmy was delighted at last to be given the opportunity to play for Scotland in his preferred position of centre forward against England at Hampden. It will be recalled that he was on the left wing in 1908, had been strangely omitted in 1906, and was too inexperienced in 1904. He was now almost thirty-two, and he realised that this might be his last chance to play for Scotland in the most important game in the calendar. He would be wrong in that respect, for he did reappear in 1912, but it was 1910 that he is remembered for.

As a result of the Ireland game, the writer of the *Dundee Courier* has a gloomy prognostication about Scotland's chances against England game on 2 April: 'While I would be pleased and surprised to see the Thistle emerge victors, it is a forlorn hope and the only result which can be looked forward to with any confidence is the downfall of Scotland'. This is strong, not to say treasonous stuff, but the writer goes on to say that playing Jimmy Hay at left-back is 'nothing short of an absurdity' and that Scotland's half-back line of Aitken, Thomson and McWilliam will never cope with the 'thrusts' of the Englishmen. Curiously he does not mention Quinn, yet all the fans seldom talked about anyone else.

A crowd of 106,205 (a little short of the 121,000 of two years previously) turned up at Hampden Park to see it much changed since the riot of the 1909 Scottish Cup final. A new telegraph station would be in operation to feed the eager English Press and public desperate for news of the game, and much of the stand had been rebuilt, as indeed had the surrounding wall. 284 police would be on duty, and thirty constables were detailed to escort the English charabanc from their headquarters at St Enoch's Hotel.

The game saw Scotland well on top throughout, and the two goals featured Jimmy Quinn. Erstwhile Celt Bobby Templeton set up Quinn, who charged through the full-backs and, when Hardy came out of his goal, Quinn's shot hit him but rebounded to Quinn's Celtic colleague Jimmy McMenemy, who made no mistake. Ten minutes later, Quinn once again avoided being sandwiched between the full-backs by charging through them at full speed and this time scored himself.

The description of the crowd's reaction is illuminating. 'Flags and handkerchiefs could be seen waving, whistles were shrilling and bells were ringing' as the Scottish crowd erupted at such brilliance:

> *Didn't know Quinn,*
> *Pride of the Celtic?*
> *Look here, Saxon,*
> *Where you bin?*
> *Not to know Quinn,*
> *Quinn of the Celtic?*

The Englishmen would certainly know all about him now, for he distributed the ball with genius. McMenemy was 'pure art' and Templeton did loads of back-heeling and generally played to the gallery. The much-maligned half-back line of Aitken, Thomson and McWilliam was splendid, with Peter McWilliam of Newcastle in particular singled out as 'Peter the Great'. Scotland's reverse in Ireland did not matter too much in any case, for Wales beat Ireland and thus Scotland became the British Champions again.

The Scottish Press were unanimous in their paying of homage to Jimmy Quinn, whom they occasionally called 'King James', perhaps somewhat deliberately to play to the Jacobite sympathies of Celtic fans! Great praise is given for his unselfishness: 'Quinn's game was to see that the English never troubled his partners and he carried this out admirably, staving off opponents and playing the real centre by feeding his wings and sinking his individuality.'

Even the London papers were in rhapsodies about him. The *Evening Dispatch* asks categorically 'Is there a better centre forward in the king-dom than James Quinn? If so, who is he?' Then it adds significantly (with a reference to his troubles of 1905 and 1907), 'It is wonderful how he has lived down the ill feeling of a few years ago.' The *Daily Mail*, which boasted that it included Buckingham Palace among the homes where it was delivered, is similarly impressed: 'In Quinn, they (Scotland) have undoubtedly the finest centre in the four countries – strong, resolute and dashing, sometimes opening the game up for his wings and on other occasions going through by himself, but nearly always doing the best thing possible under the circumstances'. Whether the dying King Edward VII read this is not recorded...

Other quotes refer to his jousts with his old adversary big Bob Crompton: 'His bouts with Crompton were about even. They are both of the burly order'. Others comment that 'Quinn certainly eclipsed his opposite number Wedlock' and 'His charging was something to be remembered', while he 'pivoted and passed and dashed and charged and shot to good purpose throughout', kept 'spreading the play with an impartiality beyond reproach' and showed 'clever passing and feinting'. One quote sums him up by saying 'he is playing real football now'.

It would be tempting to say that 2 April 1910 was, with Jimmy Quinn a second-generation Irishman and the undisputed hero of Scotland, the day that the Irish were accepted in Scotland. It would, however, be a facile interpretation – and a wrong one. The Church of Scotland in the 1920s, '30s and even as late as the '50s has a dismal record of intolerance and bigotry, which was picked up upon and used by all sorts of crackpots – who thus have some official justification for their racial and religious hatred. Yet there could be little doubt that Quinn's performance that day did make a statement about the Irish in Scotland. They were definitely here to stay, and were very much part of Scotland. The fading Philip

Quinn, now frail and bronchitic, watching from the stand, must have been proud of his boy that day.

The attitude of some Scottish Presbyterians towards Quinn's exploits for Scotland would be not unlike the attitude of some people in the United States to black athletes like Jesse Owens and Wilma Rudolph winning medals in the Olympic Games. It was good to share their success, but it hurt, and they would have preferred it to be one of 'their own kind'. But for most decent-minded people (who always have always outnumbered the bigots, even in the Rangers' supporting Protestant community) Quinn was the man who had beaten England in 1910 and deserved to be feted as such.

Quinn was an undisputed hero in 1910, and would be frequently used in arguments in future years in the trenches of the First World War when the subject turned to football and Englishmen and Scotsmen were together. In the play *Our Day Will Come*, the scene is set in defeated Germany in December 1918. A conciliatory Scotsman tries to cheer up the strict German lady by telling her that he does not like the Englishmen either, and loves being able to hammer them. The German frau does not understand what he is saying and asks 'Ah, is this your Villiam Vallace?'; 'Na' comes the reply from the cheery Scotsman, 'Jimmie [sic] Quinn!'

SEVEN

QUINN IN DECLINE
1910–1915

The summer of 1910 marked the zenith of Quinn. He had now won six League Championships in a row in a superb side, the Scottish Cup three times and was the proud possessor of 9 Scottish caps. He had, however, now passed his thirty-first birthday (and indeed reached his thirty-second in July 1910). Injuries were taking that much longer to heal. He was wise enough to realise that he could not go on for ever, and certainly not at that pace, but he had no reason to believe that he did not have a few years left in him.

He was delighted with the club, of course. Maley was not always an easy man to live with and had driven out one or two players, notably David McLean, Peter Somers and presently Jimmy Hay, but in Maley's eyes, Quinn could do no wrong. Maley and he had seldom had a cross word, although an amusing story is told of how one lovely summer Saturday at the Celtic Sports where athletics and cycling events were held, Jimmy and his friend Willie Loney turned up apparently having imbibed too much alcohol. Maley tore into Quinn, but Jimmy just smiled and said 'Boss, ye havenae seen Loney yet!' Maley saw the funny side of that, but he might not have, had the incident not concerned his two favourite players.

Quinn also loved the Celtic supporters. The love was, of course, mutual, but there was nothing that Quinn loved more than to see a barefooted youngster (and there were plenty of them at Parkhead) with a smile of his face because he (Quinn) had scored a goal or that Celtic had won a cup. He loved to see the banners of the brake clubs with his name and picture inscribed on them, and although he remained a modest, self-effacing man, he noted how people gave way to him on the streets of

Glasgow, nudged one another and how even well-dressed, middle-class Kelvinside ladies would say 'Good morning, Mr Quinn'.

He no doubt often wondered what life would have been like a decade ago in 1900 if he had gone to Sunderland when they were after him. They were just as mad on their football down there, he knew, and possibly in their own way just as successful – even though they had now lost out to Newcastle United. But, Jimmy being Jimmy, he loved being with his own folk – the Irish and second-generation Irish (now called the Glasgow Irish) who naturally supported his club, the Celtic.

King Edward VII died in May and that summer of 1910 also brought a blow to Quinn in his private life when his father, Philip, died on 28 July. The death certificate tells us that Philip died from chronic bronchitis with cardiac dilation, from which he had suffered for a month. There are two sad indirect comments on Irish immigration on the certificate. One is the statement that Philip was fifty-six (i.e. born around 1854). This would seem to contradict his marriage certificate, which tells us that he was thirty-three in 1874 (i.e. born in around 1841). The fact is that no-one knew exactly how old he was, and a discrepancy of thirteen years is a large one. Philip himself, meanwhile, had remained more or less totally illiterate all his life.

The other sad thing was that no-one knew the maiden name of Philip's mother. She was called Lizzie, and Philip's father was also Philip, a farm labourer (as one would have expected in rural Ireland), but apart from that, nothing is known about them. Such things are liable to happen in a pre-literate society, especially one scarred with famine, forced migration and the haughty indifference of an Imperial power.

Before Philip died, he had seen his son the toast of Scotland. He had been at Hampden that day in April when Jimmy scored the second goal for Scotland, and had watched him many times play at Celtic Park. In this respect, at least, Philip died happy. His wife Catherine would live until 1937 when she would have been a very old lady indeed – but again, no-one can actually say exactly how old!

Maley attended Philip's funeral in Kilsyth Cemetery for he had grown to know Jimmy's father. Maley, who was not without misfortunes in his own private life, was of course very sympathetic to Jimmy, but knew that the real therapy for grief comes when normal business is restored. The football season of 1910/11 was about to begin. Could Celtic win the Championship for seven years in a row?

There is, of course, a natural lifespan to great teams. They cannot continue to be great forever – and this is essential for the sake of competitive football. In the case of Maley's team, the ageing process and the departure of Peter Somers (who was never a favourite of Maley and seems to have decided in early 1910 that enough was enough) meant that Celtic were now a good, but no longer a great, team. In addition, Rangers had been developing fast and now had a far better side than they had fielded for a few years.

Celtic's League form up to the turn of the year in 1910/11 was mediocre, with 6 defeats and 5 draws. In addition, something seemed to be the matter with Quinn. He missed only two games through injury (one of them a 0-1 defeat to Rangers at Parkhead), but far too often he seemed slow and lethargic. He did have his great days – a 'dashing goal' against Dundee on Saturday 17 September; a couple of great goals against Hibs at Easter Road on the Holiday Monday of 19 September and a glorious goal against Raith Rovers at Parkhead on Hogmanay that burst the net – but far too often he was out of touch, clearly missing Somers in the same way as he missed Bennett for a while in 1908. He also suffered from the strange and premature decision of Maley to break up the immortal half-back line of Young, Loney and Hay by changing the positions of Jimmy Hay with left-back Joe Dodds.

The truth was that Quinn was now on the slide. He was thirty-two, and that is old for a striker – especially one who has over a number of years sustained a huge amount of knocks and injuries. Yet such was the talismanic quality of the very name 'Quinn' that Maley dared not drop him. It would have been foolish because there was no obvious replacement, and in any case the presence of Quinn was such that the opposition would always have two men on him, giving an opportunity for another forward to score the goals.

But the team struggled. Three of the first four games were lost, and then there was a particularly bad spell in the late autumn. A defeat in the final of the Glasgow Cup to Rangers on 8 October 1910 was perhaps the indication that the pendulum was beginning to swing to the west side of the city rather than the east. A couple of feckless 0-0 draws with Airdrie and Third Lanark followed in November, before a defeat at Dundee. It was an unfortunate one as well: Dundee scored in the last minute, then Celtic apparently equalized immediately with a through-ball from Quinn to Kivlichan, but the referee declared that it was time-up seconds before Kivlichan's shot crossed the line.

Perhaps there was another reason for Quinn's poor form. There was a bank at Charing Cross that went bankrupt in scandalous circumstances, leading to criminal charges being pressed against its proprietor, Mr Alfred William Carpenter. Such events were far from rare in 1910, but they often impoverished people who had invested heavily in them. Quinn had apparently put some of his money there, and felt compelled in late November to issue a statement to the Press via the club in which he denied that he had lost heavily. Why he did this, we do not know, but the implication of this curious business was that he had indeed lost some money. Perhaps this mysterious affair was preying on his mind and may partially explain his lacklustre performances?

But he was far from finished. December saw a rally and an improvement both in the form of Quinn and of the team in general. Quinn scored a great goal on 17 December against Kilmarnock when he 'burst through the backs, reminiscent of Quinn of old' but very few of the 5,000 crowd who watched Celtic beat Raith Rovers 5-0 on the last day of 1910 (the day that he burst the net with a shot) would have thought that this team were capable of winning the Scottish League yet again. In this they would be proved correct.

The *Glasgow Herald* shares their pessimism as it sums up 1910 and looks forward to 1911 in the context of how Scotland will do in the internationals. It bemoans the fact that there is no replacement for 'the physical and playing ability of the Celtic centre' for it adds, more in sorrow than in anger, that 'neither Quinn nor McMenemy have this year reached top form for the Celts'.

Quinn now had the pleasure of watching two other Croy boys breaking into the Celtic side... and they both had almost the same name! One was Tommy McAteer, who had now joined Celtic after putting them out of the Scottish Cup the previous season, and the other was a prodigiously talented youngster with famously thick legs, called Andy McAtee. The 1901 Census had shown that the Quinns lived at number 18 Smithston Row, and at number 20 lived the McAtee family with Andrew a twelve-year-old 'scholar'. Jimmy always felt a proprietorial interest in young Andy McAtee, who would soon, however, show that he needed no such protective influence.

1911 opened with a creditable draw against Rangers at Ibrox, and then the Croy boys of Quinn and McAtee scored the goals against both Clyde and Partick Thistle, raising hopes that a challenge might yet be made for the Championship. Alas, it proved a false dawn as Celtic lost at Aberdeen, and Celtic's challenge gradually fizzled out in a series of insipid draws.

The problem was the forward line. Quinn was definitely out of touch, suffered repeatedly from injuries and was not even realistically considered for the Scotland games. McMenemy too suffered a loss of form, and hard though the earnest John Hastie worked at inside left, he was no Peter Somers. Andy McAtee looked promising, and had a cannonball shot, but as yet lacked experience. Credit must also be given to Rangers, who had a good season and deserved their first League triumph for almost a decade.

But Quinn had a good Scottish Cup. It was he who scored the vital goal against Aberdeen in the semi-final on 11 March to set up a Cup Final (Celtic's fourth in five years) against Hamilton Accies, who had played well to defeat Dundee in the other semi. Peter Somers in fact was now with Hamilton, but suffering so badly from injuries that he was on the verge of retirement. It was generally expected that with Quinn now apparently back in form, Celtic would comfortably beat the lowly Lanarkshire men. Quinn now also had a point to prove regarding the international scene. The week before the Scottish Cup final, Scotland had drawn 1-1 with England at Goodison Park with Willie Reid of Rangers now in the centre forward spot. Quinn felt that he was better than Reid, even at the age of thirty-two.

The Scottish Cup final at Ibrox on 8 April 1911 was watched by 46,000 and generally agreed by most to be one of the worst of them all. The pitch was dry and hard, Hamilton were overawed and Celtic failed to take the initiative and win the game, with Quinn in particular showing a lack of understanding with inside forward John Hastie. (Perhaps the most interesting thing about this game was the fact that both teams had an inside left called Hastie!)

The replay the following week was a different matter. Heavy rain (welcome after the drought) an hour-and-a-half before the start cut the attendance to about 25,000 and the wind was just as strong as the previous week. Crucially, Hastie was dropped, Kivlichan moved to inside left and Andy McAtee brought in on the right wing. Celtic played into the western gale in the first half with Quinn claiming (with a touch of hyperbole) that he could hardly breathe for the wind, and the score stayed at 0-0 at half-time. But the second half saw Celtic rally with the wind, and then Quinn and McMenemy teamed up well (they had rarely done so that season) for a truly magnificent goal.

It was McMenemy who started it all, passing to a few men and getting the ball back as he began a mazy run on goal. He reached the edge of the penalty area, drew back his foot as if to shoot, then suddenly withdrew, leaving Quinn to rush in and score a pile-driver from the edge of the area, catching everyone by surprise. It was clearly a well-rehearsed move, but it was all the more effective for never having been seen before in public.

Celtic were now on easy street with the strengthening wind behind them, and Quinn was delighted when Tommy McAteer, his friend from Croy, scored the second at full time. Tommy had narrowly missed out the previous year when with Clyde, who had lost to Dundee after three games in the final. But the Scottish Cup of 1911 was a Croy triumph, for a key factor in determining the improvement of Celtic from the first game was the introduction of young Andy McAtee. Banners were hung out of windows in Croy that night, extolling the virtues of McAtee, McAteer and Quinn. Indeed it was a remarkable achievement that a village the size of Croy could produce three members of a team that won the Scottish Cup.

That was some compensation for the loss of the League, but Jimmy's season finished on a sour note. He had played well to beat Third Lanark 5-2 and earn Celtic a place in the Glasgow Charity Cup final against Rangers at Hampden on Wednesday 10 May. Celtic had acquired a new amateur centre forward called Willie Nichol from Aberdeen and, to try him out in the centre forward position, Quinn agreed to move to the left wing. This exposed him to the fierce tackling of Campbell and Gordon, and Jimmy was badly lamed in both legs. He had to limp off (hardly for the first time in his career) in the sixty-fifth minute and the damage to his legs was so bad that he immediately declared himself out of Celtic's projected summer tour of Germany, Austro-Hungary and Switzerland.

Quinn thus spent his thirty-third birthday in July 1911 slowly recovering from injury in circumstances cruelly reminiscent of his first great season of 1904. The difference was that he was now seven years older and thus less likely to heal so quickly. Increasingly, it was being put to him by his wife and family that his football days would end soon, and that, before he was crippled for life, a dignified retirement was in order. Jimmy laughed

at this and said that he still had a year or two left in him. He was determined, injuries or no injuries, to keep going because he still loved the
game, the Celtic and the companionship that football brings. In any case,
the alternative was almost certainly the mines and it was difficult for anyone to convince him that hewing coal was in any way a more healthy or
salubrious way of earning a living than professional football.

But the injuries took their time and, between the start of the season and 2 December 1911, Jimmy played in only two games. One was
against Clyde on 2 September when he scored two magnificent goals,
and the other was a week later in a Glasgow Cup game against Partick
Thistle. Early on and without being aware of what he had done, Jimmy
aggravated one of these injuries and was put on to the left wing for the
rest of the game. In a match characterised by some terrible football, the
final score was 3-3, and Quinn's absence from the replay ensured that a
feeble Celtic went down 0-3.

Quinn's absence during October and November was significant
in that Celtic stuttered and stumbled, losing to Hamilton Accies and
Rangers, drawing some games and scraping through to a victory in others. Goals simply did not come as Maley experimented with Nichol,
Donaldson and Travers. McMenemy was out as well from mid-October,
and little went right for Celtic, whose impatient and intolerant fans con-
tinually indicated their disapproval.

The date 2 December 1911 saw a game at Parkhead against St Mirren.
It would turn out to be a very significant day in the history of the club,
for it was Patsy Gallacher's debut and the return of Jimmy Quinn. Quinn
reputedly made a comment about how Maley would be done for man-
slaughter if he put the apparently underfed and puny Gallacher out to
play. It is hard to imagine the kindly Jimmy being so insensitive, and the
story does have all the hallmarks of a subsequent invention. In any case,
Jimmy immediately spotted some talent in the diminutive Irishman and
gave him all the encouragement and support that he could.

Jimmy was glad to be back and played well even though he did not
score. He made up for that on New Year's Day 1912 when he scored
all three goals against Rangers at Parkhead, picking up passes and
feeds from a left winger from Fife called John Brown. The hat-trick at
Parkhead dispelled any rumours that might be circulating about Quinn
retiring and showed the world that Quinn was back. It was possibly
too late to do much about winning the League (and indeed the team's

form continued to be inconsistent) but there was still the Scottish Cup, and in any case, the Press very soon began to talk about Quinn in the same breath as a return to the Scotland side.

Jimmy would regain his place in the Scotland team in 1912. The year started off very well when Annie gave birth to her sixth child, Mary, on 7 January. Jimmy celebrated the following week with a fine goal against Motherwell, but it seems that as far as Quinn was concerned, Maley decided that the League was gone and that Quinn need not be used. Jimmy played very few League games the rest of the season due to a combination of injury and international duty. He was, as it were, kept in cotton wool for the Scottish Cup.

The Scottish Cup was an example of how a team who are not playing all that well for various reasons can nevertheless buckle down and get some success. Celtic were perhaps lucky in getting two easy ties in the early stages. Dunfermline Athletic (slow starters in Fife football and a poor side until the arrival of Jock Stein in 1960) managed to keep Jimmy quiet and restrict Celtic to 1-0 on 27 January, then Quinn scored two goals against lowly East Stirling on 10 February before organizing the great Celtic rescue at Pittodrie on 24 February.

Celtic were 0-2 down soon after half-time and looking as if they were exiting from the Scottish Cup. Quinn's young Croy protégé, Andy McAtee, had already missed a penalty, so when Celtic were awarded another (that the home fans did not think justified), he did not feel like taking another. Quinn volunteered to take it, captain Sunny Jim nodded tacitly, then, to his horror, observed goalkeeper Greig get a hand to it. But Quinn still had sharp enough reflexes and was able to get the rebound and drive home.

Celtic were now back in the game, but minutes were ticking away and Aberdeen fans were becoming optimistic that they were about to remove the mighty Glasgow Celtic from the Scottish Cup. Quinn, although tired because of the pace of the game, was still aware that it was up to him to lead the line when the ball came forward. Eventually, he saw the opportunity. A ball came to him from a defensive clearance and he noticed out the corner of his eye that Andy McAtee was unmarked on the edge of the penalty area. He whipped the ball to him, and young McAtee, who was already becoming famous for his shot, fired home to compensate for his penalty miss. Quinn was delighted for the youngster. He knew what it was like to miss a penalty.

Celtic therefore travelled south, still in the Scottish Cup. The issue was resolved two weeks later when Celtic beat Aberdeen 2-0 at Celtic Park in the replay. Jimmy fell awkwardly and wrenched his knee and had to be deployed on the left wing rather than the centre of the field. He was still influential out there, but this time it was one of the hitherto disappointing under-performers, Paddy Travers, who got the goals against the team that he (Travers) was destined to manage (not without success) after the First World War.

For the semi-final, Celtic's best available forward line of McAtee, Gallacher, Quinn, McMenemy and Brown came together to defeat the strong-going Hearts 3-0 at Ibrox on 30 March. Quinn didn't score, but played a stormer as Andy McAtee made all three goals for McMenemy (twice) and Brown.

Quinn thus had the opportunity to win his fifth Scottish Cup medal against Clyde on 6 April. It was a game played in a gale (as so many Scottish Cup finals were) and, once again, Quinn did not score, preferring to be the decoy, and allow the prodigious talents of Patsy Gallacher and Andy McAtee to pick up the masterful, visionary passes of the immortal McMenemy. The wind spoiled the game to an extent, but it was Celtic who won 2-0 with goals from McMenemy and Gallacher. Once again, Celtic had rescued the Scottish Cup from a barren League season, and Quinn now had five Scottish Cup medals.

Quinn had by this time played three international games that spring of 1912 against the English League, Wales and England. The Scottish League game against the English League was played at Middlesbrough on 17 February and Quinn had one of his rare poor games, as Scotland went down 0-2. He was still considered to be good enough, however, to play in the first international against Wales at Tynecastle on 2 March.

It was a tough game, and Quinn was fouled repeatedly by a Welsh side that had done quite well against Scotland in recent years. By half-time, Quinn was limping, had a split lip and had grazed his cheek. But, being Quinn, he kept going and eventually, in the eighty-eighth minute, it was he who scored the only goal of the game. The Scotsman's report of the game stresses how tough it was and the 31,000 Scottish crowd were 'demented with joy' at Quinn's late counter, which 'filled the Welsh cup with woe'.

Quinn's own cup of woe was also full when he missed the Ireland game through injury, but he was once again picked for the Scotland *v.* England game on 23 March. Scotland did well to get a point here in front of 127,000 fans – who somehow or other managed to get to Hampden in spite of there being a rail strike. This was a crazy team selection. Scotland took the field with three centre forwards – Davie McLean (ex-Celtic) as the real centre forward, Andy Wilson at inside left and Jimmy Quinn on the left wing, having been given the remit (as in 1908) of dealing with the physical challenges of England's Bob Crompton.

The game was disappointing and Quinn, who clearly wanted to be in the centre, was 'like a square peg in a round hole'. England, the better team, missed many chances, as the game ended 1-1 to the huge disappointment of the Hampden crowd who remembered Quinn's performance when in his true position in 1910. It was to be Quinn's last international appearance for Scotland, and it was a shame that it ended like this, although a 1-1 draw was hardly a disaster and earned Scotland a share in the International Championship.

There was some recompense in the annexing of the Scottish Cup (already described) and Quinn had the satisfaction of winning the Glasgow Charity Cup as well… although the meaning of the word 'winning' has to be somewhat elastic. Celtic had reached the final thanks to goals from Quinn and Gallacher in a game against Queen's Park. This set up a final against Clyde, giving Clyde the opportunity for some revenge for their Scottish Cup final defeat. Twenty-five thousand saw a dull game with no goals, but it suited Celtic. The decision had been taken that there would be no replay as it was now 11 May and there was little appetite for further football as the players were needing their close season. Indeed the sporting pages of the newspapers were now filled with the Stockholm Olympics.

The Charity Cup was to be decided on the basis that corner kicks would be counted. This was, of course, meat and drink for the experience of Quinn and McMenemy, who were able to win corners by earning deflections off an opponent's foot and, as long as Celtic's miserly defence did not concede a goal, this would suffice. It was, however, an odd way for the great Jimmy Quinn to win his last ever winners' medal! That summer of 1912 Quinn had his last tour with Celtic – this time to Denmark in early June. It was a short trip of only a fortnight, sailing from Hull and playing five games, including a game against each of the

Danish and Norwegian Olympic teams. It was light-hearted stuff, and Jimmy kept scoring the goals, eight in total over five games.

The 1912/13 season was a disappointing one for Celtic and the campaign that told Jimmy Quinn that the end of his career was in sight, although there had been a few straws in the wind (usually in the shape of injuries that took longer and longer to recover from) before then. It could not really be said that Celtic were a bad team – and indeed it was not an entirely barren season, for they won the Glasgow Charity Cup at the end – and they had promising youngsters like McAtee, Gallacher and Johnstone. But Celtic had wretched ill luck with injuries to their older, more experienced players with McMenemy, Loney and Quinn all out for long stretches of the season.

In Quinn's case, however, it was obvious that he was slowing down permanently. He was still capable of scoring great goals – in fact there was still no-one better than he – but it is noticeable that in newspaper reports of his performances (even in papers like the *Glasgow Herald* and the *Glasgow Observer*, which used to idolise him) words like 'dash' and 'speed' appeared far less often.

The season had barely started when he wrenched his knee and had to go off. The annoying thing was that it happened in a benefit match – Celtic loved to play such games in the early part of the season as glorified practice games – for a Vale of Leven player called Archie Long. The pain was excruciating, and even Quinn, famed for his stoicism and ability to play through the pain barrier, could not limp about on the wing and had to go off. This was on 20 August 1912 and he was out for over a month until 28 September. It began to be feared that an operation might be necessary.

In the event, it wasn't – at least not yet – and Quinn's return coincided with the start of the Glasgow Cup campaign, in which Quinn might have hoped to add another medal to his tally of five. For a while it looked possible. In the semi-final against Clyde at Shawfield, 22,000 saw Quinn beat three men before shooting from just inside the penalty area to score Celtic's second goal of four. The *Glasgow Observer*, enthusiastic as always, says that the applause was still reverberating around the ground (and frightening the birds) a good two minutes after the game had restarted.

A huge crowd came to Hampden to see the Old Firm Glasgow Cup final. It may even be that the records were broken for a Scottish club game that day, for the gates were rushed and it was impossible to say with any degree of certainty how many people were inside, although 80,000 seems probable. Quinn opened the scoring on the half-hour mark, but Celtic lost Loney through injury and Rangers gained the upper hand to win 3-1. McMenemy was out with a broken arm, and without his senior colleague, Quinn was unable to get going for a counterattack.

This would turn out to be Quinn's last final, and in the Scottish League, Celtic now began to struggle, losing games to Raith Rovers and Motherwell for example. They did, however, gain a modicum of revenge for the Glasgow Cup final defeat when they got the better of Rangers by the odd goal in five at Parkhead on 25 October. Quinn passed to Brown for the first, had a hand in the second (which Patsy Gallacher finished off) and then scored a brilliant winner as he rampaged through the Rangers defence, leaving three men floundering in his wake.

Quinn was also unwittingly responsible for an opponent losing the sight of an eye. This was at Parkhead on 9 November, when the luckless Tom Hegarty of Hearts got in the way of Quinn's foot as he tried to control a ball that was falling behind him. Hegarty took a kick in the face, and the end result was a detached retina that meant that the poor man could only see out of one eye for the rest of his life. Quinn was distressed at this, and although Hegarty publicly absolved Quinn from responsibility, Quinn always felt that he was in some way to blame.

Celtic finished 1912 and began 1913 well. Quinn headed the only goal of the game at Ibrox in the closely fought New Year Day game, and by mid-January Celtic had briefly regained top spot in the League. Yet the sparkle had gone, and games were being won by only the odd goal. Gallacher was brilliant, but could not yet be expected to be consistently so, and it was now very obvious that Quinn was slowing down.

The team lost to Hibs on 18 January, then only drew with Airdrie on 25 January as Quinn sustained a recurrence to his knee injury. He was out for the game on 1 February, ill-advisedly returned for an easy Scottish Cup match against Arbroath and had to retire injured yet again. Then without Quinn, Celtic surrendered 0-3 to Aberdeen at Pittodrie, thereby losing the initiative in the League race to Rangers – something that they never regained that year.

Quinn, in addition to his intermittent knee problem, seemed also (more worryingly) to have 'incessant headaches' – something that may have been caused by heading a heavy, muddy football. The date 8 March at Parkhead saw 66,000 to see the Scottish Cup tie with Hearts. Quinn was clearly out of sorts as the Edinburgh men surprised everyone by winning 1-0 to put Celtic out of the competition. He was similarly unimpressive the next two weeks when Celtic lost two League games to Motherwell and Falkirk to knock them out of the League race as well.

He then confounded those who said he was finished by scoring a hat-trick against Raith Rovers on Monday 24 March, all of them well taken goals, but then on Saturday 29 March, at home to Kilmarnock, sustained a further aggravation to his knee after scoring a good goal. His only other contribution to the season was a goal in a friendly against Alloa, for he subsequently ruled himself out of further games. He was suffering so much pain.

It was probably at this point in the summer of 1913 that he seriously considered retirement for the first time. He discussed the matter with Maley, pointing out that he would be thirty-five in July and did not have very much left in him anyway, even without the problem to his knee, which now seemed to be injured whenever he played. But Maley managed to persuade him to stay on for another year, even if it meant an operation on his knee, pointing out to him that he would still be a valuable influence in the dressing room and behind the scenes.

In any case, there was still no obvious successor to Quinn. True, Barney Crossan had scored a marvellous goal in the Glasgow Charity Cup final, but whether he was a long-term replacement had yet to be seen. Maley was convinced that the 1912/13 season had been a regrouping season. Another great team was about to emerge, and Maley wanted Quinn still to be part of it. Quinn knew that his wages as a football player were still a great deal better than those of a miner – even though it would only be for a limited period – and he agreed to another year.

It would indeed be a great year for Celtic, but Quinn's part in it would be minimal. The season started without Quinn in the first team, for a genuine goalscorer seemed to have been found in Barney Connolly, who scored in the first three games. A couple of defeats in early September in which Connolly missed chances caused Maley to recall Quinn for the game against Morton at Cappielow on 20 September. He ran out to a great ovation and delighted his fans by scoring two goals in the 4-0 beating of the Greenock side, but shortly after scoring the second goal, he was seen to limp badly and had to withdraw to the great dismay of all concerned.

It seemed that the problem was fluid on the joint of his right knee, and an operation seemed the only way of dealing with that condition. At the end of October, he went into Glasgow Infirmary for surgery amid dire predictions that he might never walk again if he did not have this problem seen to. This was, of course, alarmist talk, but it was a serious injury, and one that was imperilling what remained of Jimmy's career.

The operation went well and Quinn was soon out, being seen back at Celtic Park walking with a crutch and then a stick as he convalesced. He did not feel himself in the least threatened by any of his possible successors and was very willing to talk to them and give them tips. In addition to Barney Connolly, Celtic tried George Whitehead and Ebenezer Owers, before finding Quinn's true successor in Jimmy 'Sniper' McColl, whom they had signed from St Antony's Juniors.

Enforced leisure gave Jimmy more time for the simple pleasures of life, like a game of dominoes with fellow miners from Croy, and he was of course at home when Annie produced another baby, a girl called Margaret on 28 December 1913. His family was growing up – Sarah, the eldest, was now ten. Jimmy enjoyed his children. He was a family man. Margaret's birth certificate showed that they were still living in Barbegs House, Croy – a block of flats, now long demolished. The flat would not be enough for his family, and he would in a few years time move to Coronation Row.

As his leg improved, Jimmy showed his value to the team in acting more or less as Maley's assistant, for he was one of the few men that the manager really trusted. Quinn appeared for every game, helped with the boots, carried the hamper off the train at the railway station, talked to the players, encouraged Patsy Gallacher and calmed him down when the occasionally prickly and volatile young Irishman showed a little insecurity. On away trips he acted as Celtic's public relations man, of scarcely less value to the team off the field than on it.

One occasion, on 17 January 1914, Jimmy had to act as guide, philosopher and friend to young Andy McAtee. The team were waiting at Buchanan Street Station about to embark for Dundee when a telegram arrived for Mr McAtee. It contained the sad news that Andy's father, Peter, had been killed that morning in the mist and darkness when he was hit by a train while crossing the railway at Croy on his way to work. Quinn, though himself distressed by the news, immediately took charge of the situation and took Andy home to deal with the tragedy, while the team went on to Dundee and won 1-0.

Quinn had to a certain extent conquered his social problems of shyness and willingly talked to anyone and everyone about football. When the team visited Forfar, for example, in the Scottish Cup on 21 February, the locals were amazed to see the great Jimmy Quinn carrying the hamper, clay pipe in mouth, off the train and talking to the gawping-mouthed locals just like an ordinary man about football, operations, sore legs, the weather, local industry and whatever.

But in the one game that he played that season after his operation, he received a severe setback. Celtic had drawn against Clyde at Shawfield in the Scottish Cup on 7 February. It had been a 0-0 draw and Ebenezer Owers had been unimpressive. Maley decided that, given Quinn's good record against Clyde, he might be just the man to win the replay now that he was back in training.

Alas, it was about a month too soon. Celtic did win the replay on the following Tuesday, courtesy of two Patsy Gallacher goals, but Jimmy was obviously weak on his right leg, painfully slow and even lacking any confidence to put weight on his right leg. He hobbled off, delighted that the team had won, but wondering whether this was his last game for his beloved Celtic.

He wasn't even able to play in friendly games, nor go on the Central European Tour in the summer, but he did work hard at his walking, running and exercises. He enjoyed the success of the team who won a League and Cup double and was delighted to see Jimmy McMenemy of Celtic and Willie Reid of Rangers score the goals for Scotland that beat England at Hampden in April.

He had decided that he might give it one last go the following season if his leg improved enough, but progress was slow. He did not really feel that he could last the pace of full-time football with Celtic for another season and he toyed with the idea of going part-time and playing for the likes of East Stirling or Stenhousemuir, who were apparently interested in him. Alternatively, he could rejoin Smithston Albion or the new team that had appeared called the Croy Celtic. He was so busy getting himself fit that he barely noticed that the heir to the Austro-Hungarian throne had been murdered in Sarajevo at the end of June. It was only at the end of July that Jimmy and the rest of the world woke up to the fact that politicians and diplomats were talking very seriously about a major European war.

On 1 August 1914, with the world only days away from the First World War cataclysm that was to destroy so much about what had gone before, there was another clear indication that things were about to change. Celtic's great success in 1914 had been achieved with Quinn playing in only two games and it was obvious that retirement at the age of thirty-six was inevitable. A poem appeared in the *Glasgow Observer* as the rest of the world worried about the shelling of Belgrade by the Austro-Hungarians and the mobilization of the Russians and the Germans. The poem went:

JIMMY QUINN, THE OLD WARHORSE

Say, Jimmie, that it is not true
That you must quit the game.
For we are Oh so proud of you
And glory in your fame.
Far be the day when we must part
Ne'er see these runs of thine
They spread dismay in many a heart
And oft enraptured mine.

Your name is known from pole to pole,
Full many an exile sighs,
In fancy sees some thrilling goal
You scored in 'Paradise'.
We cannot spare you, 'lad o' parts',
Our daring, dauntless boy,
The idol of all Celtic hearts –
Jimmie Quinn from Croy.

Jimmy had not officially retired at that stage, for his name appears in the Celtic retained list for 1914/15, but circumstances compelled his semi-retirement. Shortly after the declaration of war, it was decreed that no full-time professional football was to be allowed and that anyone who was to play part-time professional football must also work in the munitions or essential industries, or join the forces.

In Jimmy's case, this meant a return to the pits in Croy, probably the one called Number 3 Pit across the road from where he would soon live in Coronation Row, but he agreed with Maley that he would do some training and could be called upon on an ad hoc basis, if required. He probably did not really consider joining the forces. He was thirty-six (not quite too old, but old enough) and, in any case, young men from mining districts were not submitted to the same psychological pressure to join up as elsewhere, in that the production of coal was seen as paramount to the British war effort.

So, to the pits Jimmy returned. In fact he played 6 times for Celtic in the strange circumstances of the 1914/15 season, normally on occasions when Sniper McColl was injured. For example, he had a three-week spell in October, during which time he looked overweight and suffered from problems with his knees – a problem exacerbated by the amount of bending and kneeling one is obliged to do down a pit. Yet he scored a late winner for Celtic against Hamilton Accies on 24 October, and in the Old Firm League game a week later took a free-kick that the Rangers goalkeeper could only parry to Patsy Gallacher.

On 30 November, he had a sad duty to perform in carrying the coffin of the great inside left Peter Somers, who, along with McMenemy, frequently rejoiced in the title of 'Quinn's fetch and carry men'. Peter had died after an unsuccessful attempt to amputate part of his leg for blood poisoning, and Jimmy was distraught at the loss of his close friend. Indeed, the world was changing as he saw his other friends at the graveyard that day. Peter had gone at the age of thirty-six and the newspapers were making grim reading and confirming the impression that this war would definitely not be over by Christmas. Already Croy and Kilsyth had lost some men from the regular army in France. How many more young men would Jimmy see buried before their time?

In December he was twice summoned by Maley and he rewarded his old boss by scoring twice against Queen's Park and once against Hamilton. Yet he suffered after both games from pains in both legs and other muscular problems. He played in only two more games. He scored a hat-trick in a friendly against Belfast Celtic on 23 January (a Saturday where normally a Scottish Cup tie would have been played – but that tournament, like internationals, had been cancelled for the duration). His final game was against Hearts at Parkhead on 30 January before a crowd of 55,000 – at least 10,000 of whom were wearing khaki as they were home on leave or Englishmen stationed in Scotland and availing themselves of an opportunity to see this mighty man called Quinn.

The game ended 1-1, with Hearts given a great ovation by the Celtic crowd in view of their many enlistments to the colours. It was a fast, good game, but Jimmy was injured yet again and came to the conclusion by the end of it that he no longer had the speed for first-class football. His Croy friend Andy McAtee got Celtic's goal, and he was delighted at that.

'Sniper' McColl was not injured again for the rest of the season. Quinn was therefore not needed, and the decision was taken that Jimmy was hanging up his boots. There would have been greater notice taken of this event, had the country not been involved in matters of far graver importance.

EIGHT

QUINN IN RETIREMENT
1915-1945

The last thirty years of Jimmy Quinn's life were hardly retirement in the conventional meaning of the word. His time was spent basically doing three things. One was digging coal, another was bringing up his family, in whom he was very proud, and the other was following football, and in particular his one and only love within the game – Glasgow Celtic. Unlike some other ex-Celts, he did not leave with any bitterness towards Willie Maley and was welcomed back at Celtic Park as often as he wished. Indeed, he was frequently asked for his advice, a trend that became more apparent when his old friend Jimmy McMenemy appeared at Celtic Park as trainer in the mid-1930s.

Quinn was not cut out for football management, and he never sought any such position. A football manager requires a high profile, something that did not suit Jimmy. He far preferred the miners' rows in his native village of Croy, where he could talk with and work with his friends. Often on a Saturday during the season, Quinn would be seen heading off to the station to catch the train to see the Celtic, but otherwise he seldom strayed very far away from his native heath.

His trips to Celtic Park, however, were the highlight of his week. Like most Scotsmen, ninety minutes on Saturday afternoon were 'the revenge on the rest of the week'. In particular he would have been glad to see the gradual emergence of a successor to himself. Maley inadvisedly unloaded Sniper McColl in 1920, believing that he had the natural successor to Quinn in the 'Boy Wonder' Tommy McInally. Alas, Tommy.

although in no way lacking ability, proved to be unable to cope with the emotional demands of playing for Celtic – and in any case turned out to be a better inside forward.

Then there was the brief hour of glory of Joe Cassidy in 1923, before there emerged from the deprived streets of Garngad in Glasgow a youth with the same sort of physique, the same courage and the same ability to take a goal as Quinn himself. Like Quinn, this young man lacked self-confidence, at least in his early years, but Quinn was encouraged by Maley to talk to the earnest young Jimmy McGrory and gee him up. This Quinn would do, and the results were phenomenal. In addition, for a while Quinn still had his old teammates in Andy McAtee and Patsy Gallacher to cheer on as well. Even when their careers ended, Quinn kept up his connections with the team, appearing as linesman in testimonial games, notably that of Jimmy McGrory when he did the honours along with Alan Morton of Rangers, and being happy to be photographed with the team in 1937 after they had won the Scottish Cup.

For Celtic, the inter-war years are generally agreed to have been a poor period. There were some great moments, particularly in Scottish Cup finals and famously in the all-Britain Empire Exhibition Trophy of 1938, and certainly Celtic had many fine players, but it was Rangers who picked up most of the League Championships. Indeed Rangers might have won nine in a row long before Jock Stein's Celtic did, had it not been for the excellent Motherwell team of 1932.

But the Celtic retained the love and affection of its fans, not least Jimmy Quinn who was now proud to call himself a fan. Jimmy was genuinely upset by the comparative lack of success of the team but re-fused to compare the side unfavourably with his own great team. Very seldom would anyone hear a sentence beginning with 'In my day...' He developed a genuine liking for McGrory and no one clapped or cheered louder than Quinn when McGrory scored his famous goals or broke yet another record.

There was one dreadful day in Celtic's history which would have af-fected Jimmy deeply. It was of course 5 September 1931, when Celtic goalkeeper John Thomson was killed after an accidental collision with Rangers' Northern Irish centre forward Sam English. Jimmy of course had been famous, even notorious, for the way he treated goalkeepers, with his shoulder-charging and so on. Goalkeepers were frequently hurt, occasionally seriously, but the Thomson case is one of the very few fatalities that have ever occurred on a football field. How ironic it was that this was a totally accidental collision for which the referee, quite rightly, did not even award a free kick!

John Thomson was a similar lad to Jimmy Quinn. Quiet, unassuming, unpretentious, shy, from a small mining village – in Thomson's case Cardenden in Fife. Quinn would have known what that tragedy did to Cardenden. Quinn would have wept too at the hideous death of this young man who, when introduced to Quinn shortly after joining the club in 1926, blushed and stammered at the sight of this god. Little did John know that the 'god' was equally bashful!

There were happy days as well. 1925 saw Patsy Gallacher, some thirteen and a half years after he had played his first game alongside Quinn, score his famous goal in the Scottish Cup Final in which he somersaulted into the net with the ball wedged firmly between his legs! Then the winner came from a beautiful McGrory diving header, the sort which Quinn himself might have scored, even though he was not quite so famous for headed goals as he was for other sorts.

Then there was the great year of 1938, the Silver Jubilee of the club. The dinner was held only a matter of days after Celtic had lifted the Empire Exhibition Trophy, and of course Jimmy Quinn was there to meet some of his old comrades. Willie Loney, Eck McNair, Jimmy McMenemy and Alec Bennett were all there, but Quinn would have missed the company of Peter Somers and Sunny Jim Young, great friends of his who had been removed by premature death. But of course the old man himself, Willie Maley, then aged seventy and revelling in the team that he had made and the great players that he had brought to this institution called Celtic Football Club, was still very much alive.

Of Quinn's personal life after retirement little is known. This is hardly surprising, for he did very much keep his head down and live as normal and mundane a life as circumstances would allow. The situation in 1915 when he retired from football permitted no unemployment. Great Britain needed every ounce of coal that could be hewn. Hours were long, there was the ever-present threat of a cave-in, work was not very pleasant but wages were tolerably good and in some ways the village of Croy seemed to be spared some of the worst horrors of the war. But Croy, like everywhere else, had its share of young men who went to France or elsewhere and did not return, as a glance at the beautiful war memorial in the grounds of the RC church will indicate.

Quinn was glad that he was too old and his family too young to take an active part in that war. The family would be less lucky in the Second World War. He was, however, very upset at the news of the death of Celtic footballers Peter Johnstone (who died at Arras in May of 1917) and Donnie McLeod (who died in Flanders in October of that year). Quinn had known and played with both of these men, but such was the scale of the carnage that no team could claim a monopoly of suffering or loss. Such things transcended football.

Little historical evidence exists about the reaction of Croy to the events of Dublin in 1916. British propaganda will say that the Easter Rising had little support even in Dublin itself and that it was merely the work of a few fanatics. This is not entirely true, for there was a great deal of support for the rebellion, particularly in working-class areas of Dublin. How the Irish community in Scotland reacted to the news is not clear, but the probability is that the Rising was reported in such a biased way in the British Press that it would have been hard to work out what was happening, let alone support any rebels.

But the British Press was not able to gloss over the brutal repression of the Rising, the executions and the subsequent reign of terror imposed by Black and Tan convicts. In particular, the story of a Scotsman who had to be put into a chair so that he could be shot by the forces of the strongest power on earth would have been hard to explain away. It was just as well for the British Government that any unrest did not spread to any significant extent to Croy and other such places in Scotland. It was just as well that the Irish community in Scotland concerned themselves more about their football team, who won two games in one day in 1916 and carried off the League Championship for the third year in a row.

Quinn's family kept increasing. There were to be three further additions: John was born on 25 February 1916, Anthony on 6 April 1918 and Elizabeth on 17 January 1921. By the time of Antony's birth, the family had moved into a comparatively large house in Coronation Row. This street (or a part of a street) had been built in 1901 to be ready to greet the Coronation of King Edward VII.

In 1901, these houses were considered to be new and modern. This row still exists. There were twelve of the Quinn family – Jimmy, Annie and ten children – and to us, 100 years later, it is a matter of amazement that there was enough space for such a large number. Running water was not available in these houses until about 1948, and outside dry toilets were the order of the day, with the waste lying among the cinders from the coal fire until it was collected.

Armistice Day in 1918 brought an end to the increasingly pointless slaughter in France and elsewhere. It was hardly the end of the problem for Ireland, however, and Croy people would have been appalled to hear of the Black and Tans, the bombings and the murders that went on until the Civil War was eventually settled in 1923. Scotland was not exempt from the Irish problems, for there was the 'Father McRory' chain of events in Glasgow in 1921. Ireland now had some sort of freedom in its Irish Free State, but there had been a certain amount of sweeping under the carpet of problems by the British Government, and the issue would not entirely go away.

One of Jimmy's great teammates met his death in a motorcycle accident in 1922. This was the mighty Sunny Jim Young, latterly the captain of the team until injury forced him into retirement. Quinn and Young's careers had run almost parallel, and the pair of them were great friends. Quinn was naturally distressed at this event, but it was a common accident in the 1920s (cars and roads were far more dangerous than they are now, and there were no strict regulations about the wearing of crash helmets).

Trouble was also brewing on the horizon for the mining industry and for Croy in particular. The end of the war meant that subsidies were reduced and indeed the demand for coal dropped, so that the employers were contemplating reducing pay and lengthening the day. Such an attitude pushed a hitherto very compliant and docile workforce rather too far, and in 1921 there was a serious, although short-lived coal strike, in which troops were deployed by a jittery Government afraid of a British version of what had happened in Russia in 1917. The Kilsyth and Croy area had seen troops billeted in Stirling Castle to keep an eye on the area, baton charges by police, mass demonstrations and many arrests. Quinn would have been very much involved in this.

The Miners' Strike – or as some would call it a 'lock-out' in that the coal owners were again attempting to reduce wages and lengthen the day – began in 1926. For two weeks in early May 1926, the issue was complicated by a General Strike in which the entire Trade Union Movement supported the miners, but solidarity soon collapsed and the miners were compelled to stay out alone until autumn 1926, before sheer starvation forced a surrender. For the local area, we have an excellent pamphlet called *The Miners of Kilsyth in the 1926 General Strike and Lockout* by Paul and Carol Carter detailing such things, for example, as what happened to the luckless John Heeps of the Communist Party. Because at a public meeting he said 'Three cheers for Lenin, three cheers for McLean, down with the red, white and blue and up with the red flag', he was sentenced to three months' hard labour in Barlinnie Jail!

Sectarianism was at least put on the back burner for a while as both communities suffered equally, but it was not entirely absent. Local union leaders James Doherty, Charles Docherty, Bob Callaghan and Dan Taggart were Roman Catholics, but were totally supported by the Protestant miners from Kilsyth. A Presbyterian minister, however, called the Revd Duncan Cameron claimed that his daughter was threatened in her car by 'a band of men, mainly Irish' and blamed James Doherty for it.

Whatever nest egg that had been accumulated in Quinn's football career would surely have been dissipated in the struggle to feed a family during that dreadful year of 1926. Croy was, of course, solidly behind the strike. What happened after the surrender at the end was even worse than the privations of the strike itself. The mine owners, feeling (correctly) that they would have the Government and public opinion on their side, victimised those who had been the ringleaders during the strike and kept wages down to as low as they possibly could. Croy, being more or less completely Irish and Catholic, would hardly have escaped the revenges of the vindictive capitalist class, given the fact that the Church of Scotland in the 1920s kept warning about the Irish menace and the threat it represented to the Scottish way of life.

By the early 1930s, miners, of any creed or religion, would have been considered lucky to have a job at all, given the general collapse of industry in the wake of the Wall Street Crash of 1929 and what became known as the Depression. Great faith was placed by the mining communities in the first-ever Labour Prime Minister, Ramsay MacDonald, but he proved a weak character, far too easily seduced by the trappings rather than the actuality of power, and he ended up leading a National Government, something that was seen as a gross betrayal of the working class.

Things would slowly improve by the mid-1930s but, by that time, the problem came from a revivified Germany clearly keen to have another go at world domination. Jimmy was sixty in 1938, and would in normal circumstances have expected to retire from mining at the age of sixty-five in 1943, but by the time he reached that age, the world had been at war for four years, and as much coal as possible was required from the seemingly inexhaustible Croy coalfields.

Jimmy was idle for a spell in the 1930s (as were loads of men) but towards the end of the decade, with war against Hitler looming and indeed inevitable, Jimmy regained a job, not as a coalface miner, but as a banksman at Gartshore Number 3 Pit. He would be responsible for the safety of the movement of the cages and the bogeys. He would signal with red and green lights and it would be his job to make sure that everything was safe.

Thus in his later years, Jimmy would avoid the extremes of the problems associated with coal mining in that he was not actually under the ground. But long-term health damage had been done, although he kept working until very near his death in 1945. The injuries to his legs would keep recurring, although he seldom complained and only occasionally walked with a limp. Indeed, he still could impress his fellow villagers of Croy with his athleticism. He was by no means the only ex-footballer to suffer from leg pains in old age, but Jimmy had been injured far more often and far more severely that most. As early as 1914, a friend of his called Tom Bute of nearby Kirkintilloch had told the *Weekly News* 'No man has the slightest idea of what Quinn has to endure in a match. The moment a game is over he makes instant tracks for home, and for hours his bruised legs are steeped to the knees in hot water'. Such problems with sore legs are hardly likely to have improved in later life.

Quinn remained very sociable in his own circle. He would never claim to be anything other than a Croy miner, blessed with the ability to play football and lucky enough to be given the opportunity to play it for the team and the community that he loved. Yet he had no time for those who tried to make fun of him. The story is told by his friend Dickie Pender (who now lives in Jimmy's house in Coronation Row) of how one day when Jimmy was talking about football, and a chap tried to be funny by saying things like 'Did you ever play football, Jimmy?' Jimmy simply got up, turned and left. He might have done something that he would have regretted, but chose to leave with all dignity.

He did not, however, lack a sense of humour. One day, in the wake of Celtic's great triumph in the Empire Exhibition Trophy of 1938, a group of men were discussing tactics in the 'sitting room' of the local chip shop. In walked Jimmy, and someone asked him about tactics when he played. Jimmy said the idea was for him to run at the opposing goal where between the posts stood the goalkeeper... 'But I never hit him yet!' he said ruefully.

His family grew up and did well for themselves. His daughter Annie, for example, became a schoolteacher and taught at the nearby Holy Cross School, living to a healthy old age. His mother stayed alive until 28 October 1937. She was ninety-seven when she died of myocardial degeneration and senility. One of the strengths of the close-knit mining communities, however, was that she was surrounded by sons, daughters and grandchildren when she died in her house at 61 Smithston Crescent, Croy. Unlike that of her husband, her death certificate does give some details. She was the daughter of William Dougherty and Margaret McLaughlin, she would have been born in about 1840 and thus would have been six years old when the terrible potato famine hit the Irish nation.

She may indeed have been lucky to survive, but she came to Scotland and married fellow Irishman Philip Quinn. Her life in Scotland would hardly have been luxurious or even comfortable, but she did have the satisfaction of watching her family grow up and one of them become Celtic and Scotland's centre forward. She understood little about football, but knew that it gave loads of people a great deal of pleasure in her new home. She was proud that her son became the hero of so many people. She was also given a rare tribute by Croy Celtic FC – they had to postpone their game because of her funeral in that she had seven grandsons playing for the side that day!

In September 1939, Hitler invaded Poland and the world was at war. Once again Jimmy watched young man go off to fight. His son, Anthony, for example joined the Royal Engineers and became a motor driver. Anthony would, of course, become the father of the younger Jimmy Quinn who played for Celtic in the 1960s and early '70s.

There was a less happy end to another son. John (commonly known as Jock) joined the Argyll & Sutherland Highlanders. Tragically, he was killed at the age of twenty-seven in Western Europe on 29 September 1944 as the Allies, several months past D-Day, made their attempt to enter Germany. John's battalion was involved in the Gheel Bridgehead near the Escaut Canal and their task was the protection of the recently recaptured Eindhoven to Nijmegen Road. How exactly he met his death is not known. His name is on the beautiful war memorial at Croy church and Private John Quinn no. 2990139 also appears in the Roll of Honour at the Museum of the Argyll & Sutherland Highlanders in Stirling Castle. Jimmy and Annie were devastated about this, of course, but they were hardly alone.

It was a further and perhaps fatal blow to Jimmy's deteriorating health. His last few years during the Second World War were not the most vigorous of his life in that he suffered from a heart condition called myocarditis. In 1945, with the war over and a strong and determined Labour Government now in office, Jimmy might have hoped for a few years' retirement, but coal was still very much in demand. By October, however, his health was giving him so much trouble – he was barely able to walk some mornings and (like many other miners) constantly wheezed and coughed – that he was no longer able to work. After a short illness he died at his house, 45 Cuilmuir Terrace, Croy in the early hours of the morning of 21 November 1945.

The *Glasgow Herald* which, while hardly being a pro-Celtic newspaper, always loved Jimmy Quinn, pays him a great tribute. It describes him as 'strong, robust and clean' and quotes Willie Maley as saying that Quinn was 'definitely the club's greatest centre forward and perhaps the greatest centre Scotland ever had' – a clear indication that Maley thought Quinn was a better player than Jimmy McGrory.

At his funeral on 23 November 1945 at the Roman Catholic church in Croy, Quinn was much praised by the local priest. His funeral was attended by Willie Maley, Patsy Gallacher, Jimmy McGrory, Jimmy Delaney and others of his own age who were still alive, notably Willie Loney and Jimmy McMenemy. There were also representatives from Rangers and other Scottish clubs, for everyone knew that a great star of Scottish football was being laid to rest that day in Kilsyth Cemetery.

His gravestone is easily located near the gate. It was not, however, erected until Celtic's Centenary Year in 1988, when the club were shamed into doing something to honour one of their greatest ever servants. It has a distinctive Celtic cross and mentions James Quinn 'of Celtic Football Club'. In the same cemetery can be found the gravestone of Andrew McAtee.

His widow and family were naturally distraught, but being tough mining folk, they got on with life. They were comforted in that very few people had anything bad to say about Jimmy. Certainly in the village, he continued to be adored. True, he had had his enemies on the field, but he had long since made his peace with them, and Annie's house at 45 Cuilmuir Terrace was frequently visited by people who had played with and against Jimmy. Annie herself lived another ten years before succumbing in July 1955 to a brain haemorrhage.

NINE

QUINN THE LEGEND

In 1968, the group Manfred Mann produced a record called 'The Mighty Quinn'. The lyrics were written by Bob Dylan and it was about a famous Eskimo called Quinn. It wasn't exactly clear what the man did, but he seemed to change the atmosphere of everyone around him:

> *Come all without, come all within*
> *You'll not see nothing like the Mighty Quinn*

It was a shame that this song had not been written some sixty years earlier and applied to Celtic's great footballer of that name. As it was, the Celtic fans willingly adopted it (indeed Jimmy Quinn, the grandson of the great Jimmy played for them at the time, as we shall discover) although they occasionally amended the words to 'you'll not see nothing like Jimmy Johnstin' (as is the way with the ever-inventive of the Celtic support).

In the late 1960s there were, of course, still a few supporters who had seen the great Jimmy, but in any case his legend lived on even among those who had not. Quite a few of the author's generation had been told about Bennett, McMenemy, Quinn, Somers and Hamilton by parents who themselves had not seen Jimmy very often. We thus envisaged, as we were put to bed by doting parents, the thickset, courageous man from Croy in the green-and-white jersey who scored a hat-trick against Rangers and a great goal against England at Hampden. Some men called Patsy Gallacher and Jimmy McGrory also featured large in our dreams. It is important to place Jimmy Quinn in the context of Celtic history.

It is more or less axiomatic that a good Celtic team must have a person-ality goalscorer. Curiously, the Lisbon Lions did not have such a man. In their case, it was *men*. The goalscoring (and it was prolific) was shared around by so many different players, although Bobby Lennox and Steve Chalmers are the players who scored the most. Bobby Lennox, in fact, is the second most prolific of all Celtic goalscorers – second only to Jimmy McGrory and way ahead of Jimmy Quinn – but Bobby's were scored over a period of about twenty years, in two separate spells at Celtic Park and at a time when Celtic played far more games. But other great Celtic teams do have and must have such a man. Indeed, it is noticeable that the poor Celtic teams of, for example, the late 1940s, the early '60s and, perhaps worst of all, the early '90s, lacked such a man.

In this respect, there are perhaps only two men in Celtic's long his-tory who can be compared with Jimmy Quinn. (Bobby Lennox, fine and valuable player though he was, is excluded from this exclusive club because he was not specifically a centre forward or striker.) One such man is Jimmy McGrory, who played from 1923 until 1938, and the other is the recent idol Henrik Larsson who joined the club in 1997 and left in 2004. It is otiose and futile to compare the records of these three Celtic superstars – Quinn, McGrory and Larsson – indeed one shrinks from doing so, because one may cause offence or diminish in some way the performances of these mighty players.

A common feature to all three, however, was their rapport with the fans. All of them had this vital and intangible ingredient – even though in the case of the two Jimmys, Quinn and McGrory, it wasn't always blatant. Henrik Larsson is no show-off either, but a small incident towards the end of his Parkhead career showed how much he was part of the fans. It was the Scottish Cup semi-final on 11 April 2004 when he had just scored an easy goal against Livingston. Two Livingston defenders had left a ball to each other to deal with, and Henrik had rushed in and with a deft flick lifted the ball over the goalkeeper and into the net. Henrik then ran to his adoring fans in the north-east corner of the ground and showed them again how he performed that flick – just in case they had missed it!

The historical context is completely different. All three joined the club when fortunes were at a low ebb and all three transformed the club for the better and brought home the trophies that are the lifeblood of the fans. Quinn arrived in 1900 and served under a young and enthusiastic manager and became part of a truly great team; McGrory had the same manager, but at a time when he was a little older, more set in his ways and perhaps less willing to adapt and bend. This meant that the actual team was not what it might have been and McGrory frequently carried on his own shoulders what was sometimes a very mediocre side. Larsson arrived in 1997 in time to save Celtic from the horrors of Rangers winning the League ten times in a row, survived some uninspiring and even downright poor management, came back from an horrendous leg break and, shortly after the turn of the century, under a fine manager, became a founder member of the third Celtic Golden Age, emulating Maley's great team of a hundred years previously and the Lisbon Lions era of Jock Stein.

Economic circumstances were vastly different. Quinn's era was one of abject poverty, which the Liberals of 1906 and the following years were gradually beginning to address. It was indeed a star-studded Government that Henry Campbell-Bannerman had, with three future Prime Ministers in Herbert Henry Asquith, David Lloyd George and Winston Churchill. The task was, however, Herculean, for decades and centuries of neglect and indifference are not all that easy to change.

Glasgow's poverty and deprivation were particularly intense, with Celtic Football Club intended to be a pillar of affluence and support for a desperately underprivileged ethnic minority. More tellingly, they were the moral rallying point, the flag-wavers and the 'feel-good factor' for their community, which badly needed some boosting.

These factors certainly still prevailed for McGrory's era. The similarity lay in the long-term poverty with the added ingredient that the Celtic supporter of that era had been forced to live through the aftermath of a dreadful war, the depression of unemployment and the build-up to another dreadful war. Larsson, on the other hand, lived and played through an era of fairly obvious prosperity (in comparative terms at least) in a stadium which, by the time he arrived in 1997, was well on its way to being one of the best in the world.

Another factor, of course, is that football lacked the European dimension until the mid-1950s, when accessible air travel made it all possible. Quinn did, of course, go on his tours with Celtic, but these were close-season, relaxed affairs in countries where the development of football lagged behind that of Scotland and England. But a strong case could be made for stating that the Scotland *v.* England international was indeed the World Cup final in Quinn's era – and it was certainly celebrated or mourned as if it were! Nowadays, this fixture no longer even exists.

Crucially, tactics were different – with Quinn's age probably being the most physical. Courage, however, is something that all good centre forwards must have, and all three possessed it, suffering all sorts of injuries. Clearly these men were the heroes of their particular age, and no point is to be gained by saying that one was better than the other.

Celtic have also had other goalscoring heroes, who for one reason or another did not last as long as Quinn, McGrory or Larsson, or whose deeds are not quite so momentous. One thinks of Sandy McMahon, Jimmy 'Sniper' McColl, Joe Cassidy, the McPhail brothers, Joe McBride, Willie Wallace, Harry Hood, Dixie Deans, Kenny Dalglish, Joe Craig, Frank McGarvey, John Hartson and Chris Sutton. These men deserve an honourable mention, even though some supporters have never found it in their hearts to forgive Dalglish for his departure to Liverpool in 1977.

Another group exists, of those who had the ability to do the mighty deeds for Celtic, but who for one reason or other seemed almost to choose not to. Tommy McInally, Charlie Nicholas, Frank McAvennie or the 'Tres Amigos' (as they were inappropriately named) of the 1990s (van Hooijdonk, Cadete and Di Canio) arguably all fall into this category. In addition there were those who, no matter how hard they tried, simply did not have the ability, or at least could not do the job for Celtic. It is one thing doing well for another team, but Celtic have their own unique demands. In this context one thinks of John Coleraine, Gerry Creaney, Tommy Coyne, Tony Cascarino, Harald Brattbakk and several others.

The point is that Celtic do need a great goalscorer. The comparison of Quinn with Larsson is apt and appropriate in that trying to imagine Celtic of 1904 to 1914 without Quinn would be the equivalent of Celtic from 1997 to 2004 without Henrik Larsson. It would be like Hamlet without the Prince, as the theatregoers would say. Larsson is the undenied hero of a generation of fans. Rewind 100 years, substitute Quinn for Larsson, and then one can get some impact of the man.

Quinn's fame spread far beyond Celtic Park. That glorious April of 1910 when he became the hero of Scotland is something that has been shared by very few. McGrory was the man who created the Hampden Roar in 1933, it was said, but one suspects that the reception given to Quinn in 1910 was no less intense. Certainly, the newspapers of 1910 are full of Quinn's praise, even the middle-class *Glasgow Herald* becoming a clear and obvious member of the Quinn fan club. It did indeed say a great deal that a second-generation Irishman could become the undisputed hero of Scotland. Bigotry against the Irish was perforce compelled to take a back seat at least for a spell, until the Church of Scotland shamefully stirred it up again in the 1920s. Had there been another Quinn around then to lead Scotland, that might not have been quite so easy.

It is important to realise that Quinn's *floruit* was very much in the early years of Celtic's history. There was no historical inevitability that Celtic would become as pre-eminent as they did. True, they had got off to a good start with a large, vocal and loyal support, they were blessed by good stewardship and management and had shown the necessary vision to build a new stadium in 1892 to contain about 70,000 or 80,000 spectators at a time when attendances rarely reached five figures. The clear intention of the building of a huge stadium was to secure for themselves the Scotland *v.* England international every second year, and thus make Celtic the natural home of Scottish football, rather than the stadia of Rangers or Queen's Park.

But there was as yet no guarantee of continuing success for the team on the park. Willie Maley was appointed secretary-manager in 1897 with the mandate to produce a great team. This he proceeded to do. He built a young team, and of course it would take time. Not until 1904 did Celtic become a great side, and of course Quinn was one of the components of the cocktail.

The six years from 1904 until 1910 established Celtic, with six League Championships in a row, as Scotland's number-one side. 'The Bould Celts', 'The Mighty Celts', 'The Tim Malloys', 'The Bhoys' swept all before them in this era. The effects on Scottish society were twofold. One was that the Irish in Scotland had their rallying point, their identity and the one thing that they could do successfully. In one way perhaps they were still an underprivileged ethnic minority, but no-one could doubt the success of their football team. It would mean that they did not have to assert their identity in other less acceptable ways, through political violence or ethnic introversion. It meant that they could hold up their heads in Scottish society.

The second thing that Quinn and his men did was to introduce the great way of playing football to Scottish society as a whole. As the song written by the late Mr Cameron says:

> *And most of football's greats*
> *Have passed through Parkhead's gates*
> *To play the game in the good old Celtic way*

There is a line in that song that says 'Gallacher and Quinn have left their mark...' – indeed they have.

But there was more to it than that. Protestants had, from the earliest days and months of the club, been welcome as players and had been welcomed by the support. Now such was the aura of Young, Loney and Hay and the mighty Jimmy Quinn that Protestants began to actually support Celtic. Granted, this was a trend that was far more apparent away from Glasgow and the immediate Clydeside area, but especially after 1910 and Quinn's glorious Hampden, there was no greater role model for all of Scotland, both Protestant and Catholic, than Jimmy Quinn.

Mention has been made of Jimmy's grandson, another Jimmy Quinn, who played for Celtic from 1963 until 1974. He had been called by Celtic historians Jimmy Quinn III, but really he should be Jimmy Quinn II. He was the son of Jimmy's youngest son, Anthony, and was born on 23 November 1946, a year and a couple of days after his illustrious grandfather died.

This young man was no bad player, but was always likely to suffer for two reasons. One was that he would always endure unfair comparisons with the great Jimmy Quinn, but the other reason was that he was unfortunate in that his time at Parkhead coincided with a great era in Celtic's history when there were so few opportunities to break into the first team with so many other great players around. Sadly, he never quite made it to superstar status in the way that Dalglish and McGrain, for example, did.

He was, however, one of the 'Quality Street Kids' as they were called – the youngsters whom Jock Stein developed at the same time as his great team was winning immortality for themselves in Lisbon and elsewhere. As well as McGrain and Dalglish, there were Macari, Hay, Connelly, Davidson and many others who went on to do well in the game. Stein saw some value in Quinn and gave him a first-team spot in several tour games abroad before bringing him on as substitute in, of all games, the Old Firm at the New Year of 1968.

It was an unfortunate game to be a debutant in, for it was the infamous occasion on which two goalkeeping errors allowed Rangers an undeserved point. Quinn had little opportunity to make an impact, but he did score a wonderful goal at Kilmarnock on 2 March 1968 (and one that would have done credit to his grandfather) in another substitute appearance.

From then on, his appearances were sporadic. He was out on loan to Clyde for a spell (being unwittingly involved, while playing for Clyde against Celtic, in the incident that finished the career of the great Ronnie Simpson), but even after his return, he never really commanded a permanent spot. His problem, in sense, was his versatility. Family tradition seemed to mark him out as a centre forward, but he could play in the midfield or even as full-back. Indeed it was as full-back that he played in his only really big occasion for Celtic. This was the League Cup final of 24 October 1970, and it was an unfortunate day in that Rangers, contrary to all predictions, won the League Cup by a solitary goal. It could not be said that Jimmy had a bad game, but he was sadly associated with the defeat that gave Rangers their first trophy for four-and-a-half years.

Young Jimmy kept plugging away, playing 9 times in both season 1971/72 and 1972/73, usually at left-back to cover for an injury to Jim Brogan. By 1974 it was recognised that his moment had passed and he drifted out of football by way of Sheffield Wednesday and Hamilton Accies. He was, of course, not the first of the Quinn family to play for Hamilton, for his great-uncle Philip played in the goal for that side before the First World War. Jimmy Quinn II also played in Australia for a spell. Sadly, he died suddenly in April 2002 at the age of fifty-five.

But let us return to the great Jimmy Quinn. With all his nicknames of 'The Iron Man', 'The Bison', 'Jimmy (or Jamie) the Silent', or, quite simply, 'Jimmy', he was arguably the best-known figure in Edwardian Scotland, clearly surpassing any stage actor, politician or anyone from any other sport. One of his more interesting nicknames was 'The Equator', perhaps given to him for his ability to knock men down and hence 'equal' or 'flatten' them, or perhaps because he was considered to be the centre of the earth. 'Jimmy' was, however, the name by which he would be universally recognised. No-one knows the origin of the Glasgow catchphrase, 'See you, Jimmy', but it is certain that there was no better known 'Glaswegian' Jimmy than the miner boy from Croy.

Even when he was Scotland's hero, Jimmy would not change his habits of simple living. He was not exactly a recluse, for he would talk to anyone he met on his daily train journeys to and from Croy and the tramcar from Queen Street Station to Celtic Park, but he certainly shunned publicity. He endorsed products like Boag's Rheumatic Rum, which eased problems of neuralgia, toothache and rheumatism, (for his tough background had taught him to collect as many pennies as he could) but was frequently embarrassed by the sight of his picture on billboards.

One of his nicknames was 'The Man of a Thousand Injuries'. This was because he was frequently seen to be limping as he made his way back to Croy every night, yet would make every effort to be fit for the next game. Football was a tough game in Quinn's era – a great deal tougher than today, where referees are harder and physiotherapists are on hand to treat injury problems – but then Quinn was a tough character. Working down mines in his early days possibly taught him the value of teamwork in that one man's safety depends of the competence of another, but it also gave him courage.

Quinn knew full well that a cave-in down a mine could kill hundreds. He was also painfully aware (and indeed saw it in his own father) of the illnesses that could be brought upon miners through their unhealthy job. Life had to be faced with courage; similarly on the football field. The arena that brought a player up against characters like Nick Smith and Jimmy Galt of Rangers or Bob Crompton of England was no place for the softie. Quinn's courage lay in the fact that he could be hacked and kicked by brutal defenders – but he would come back for more, knowing that a broken leg or ankle might well be the end result. 'Never let them know you're fear'd' he would say. He could accept that fear and apprehension were a natural part of a centre forward's life, but also knew not to acknowledge this fear too openly – especially in the company of men who knew exactly how to exploit it.

It would, of course, be wrong to say that he could not dish it out as well. A tough upbringing in Croy would have taught him that he had to look after himself, and that he had to tell the world that no-one took liberties with Jimmy Quinn. But there was nothing malicious in Jimmy. He was not one of the really psychotic players who played the game then, just as they do now, with the intention of injuring. He was always willing to forgive and forget after a game and he listed some of his old adversaries from Rangers and England as his friends in later life. His manager, Willie Maley, put it rather well when he said that 'All the men that Jimmy Quinn killed are still alive!'

One aspect of the game that is illegal now and often seemed barbaric, even in Quinn's day, was the shoulder-charging of the goalkeeper. Providing that the 'keeper had his feet on the ground and that he held the ball, he could be charged by a forward using his shoulder (but not his elbow). Quinn, with his thick, broad shoulders and general speed of movement, excelled in this aspect of the Edwardian game, and many goals came from this tactic. He had the ability to barge his way through defenders without fouling them, through his sheer strength, and he revelled in the physical aspect of football. This element of the game, incidentally, lasted until well into the 1950s, certainly in Great Britain, until the climate gradually changed following pressure from the Europeans and two successive English cup finals of 1957 and 1958 when shoulder charging had a decisive and some would say an unfair effect.

But there was a great deal more to Jimmy than just the physical side of his play. He had the ability and versatility to score goals of all kinds. It is notoriously difficult to enumerate goals, for one is dependent on newspaper reports (which frequently contradict each other), but the figure frequently given for Scottish League and cup games is 216. With Glasgow Cup, Charity Cup, internationals, League internationals and friendlies, it is a great deal more. He scored fewer goals than McGrory or Larsson, but then again he played fewer games than either of them, being regularly out with injury or, on two notorious cases, with lengthy suspension.

Quinn did employ great variety in his goalscoring. His finest was often said to be the one against Kilmarnock of Christmas Day 1909, when he charged from his own half with the whole Kilmarnock defence tearing after him, and certainly an archetypal Quinn goal would appear to be in this mould. He also scored a fair few with headers from corners and free-kicks and could take a good penalty, but many of his goals simply came from the striker's art of being in the right place at the right time.

Jimmy was, of course, very fortunate in having great inside men like Jimmy McMenemy and Peter Somers and wingers of the calibre of Alec Bennett and Davie Hamilton around him. Having said that, so much of the centre forward's skill lies in the ability to read these players and be exactly where he was required to be. It is inevitable that mistakes will be made, but a feature of Quinn's play was that he was seldom seen to be at loggerheads with any of his team. A mistake would be forgiven and learned from, although he and Patsy Gallacher were reputed to be strong characters. It was perhaps just as well that the careers of Quinn and Gallacher overlapped by only a few years — otherwise there might have been a certain amount of friction, one feels.

In this respect, Quinn was an ideal team man. He was certainly no glory hunter or seeker of the limelight. He loved football, he loved Celtic and he loved Scotland. To do well for them was its own reward, although naturally his earnings and bonuses were much appreciated by the miner boy who knew what poverty was all about. He was always humble enough, like other truly great men, to know that he was lucky in his talent and that others were less so. At the railway station when the mighty Celts arrived in town, the five-year-old urchin with the ragged jersey and no overcoat shouting 'Jeemy! Jeemy! Jeemy Quinn!' would be greeted with a smile and a pat on the head.

A story is told of the time when Quinn, after his career was over, was living in Coronation Row, Croy. It must have been some time in the early 1920s when a couple of boys asked a lady, 'Which house does Quinn live in?' Politely the lady told them, but then decided to keep an eye on them lest they were up to some no good. She then to her amusement saw the two of them creep down to the Quinn house, go into his garden and steal a couple of small pebbles! This was to 'plant' them in their own garden, so that they could boast that they had a couple of stones from the garden of the mighty Jimmy Quinn.

The grandfather of current Celtic player John Kennedy was a man called Jimmy Delaney. Delaney himself became a great Celt in the years immediately before and during the Second World War, and told the story of how, as a young man starting his Celtic career, he went to see the great Jimmy Quinn in his house in Croy. The two Jimmys talked affably with each other, however much the younger one was overawed by the presence of the older one. Just as Delaney was about to leave, Quinn showed him all his medals, which he kept in a biscuit tin, and ended up by saying 'Here you are, son, just tak wan'. Such was the humility of the great Jimmy Quinn.

It is worthwhile to consider what two men say about him. One was his manager, Willie Maley, who spotted him in the early days and showed his value to the world. 'James Quinn is recognised as the greatest centre forward we have ever possessed, and we have had many fine leaders… A strong robust player possessed of a wonderful pair of shoulders which he used to great advantage and more fairly than he was given credit for. Quinn was subjected to a lot of abuse in the course of his fourteen years' service. He seldom objected to anything done to himself, but deeply resented ill-treatment to any of his colleagues less able to stand up to it, and this brought trouble on his head which was often more harsh than circumstances demanded' (*The Story of the Celtic*, published 1939).

The other is the first real history of Celtic called *The Celtic Story*, which was written by James E. Handley and published in 1960. 'With the deep chest and muscular shoulders of a charging bison he shed festoons of clinging opponents as he hurtled goalwards. He could dribble and had some outstanding solo runs to his credit, but with four forwards who knew all there was to be known about the art, he normally filled the role of rushing their passes to fruition. His left-foot shot was furious. Repeatedly it stretched the back of the net so taut that the ball rebounded into play. A hat-trick was a common achievement. The slightest opening was sufficient for him to test the goalkeeper, and even when stumbling under the attentions of the defence he could momentarily retain enough purchase to part with the ball before stretching his length on the ground. His performances on the field were so masterful that even the pencils of reporters in the ranks of Tuscany were compelled to limn [sic] his greatness in phrases like the following "Quinn, on Saturday, with all his power, dash and deadliness"; "the ever-watchful Quinn, ready to spring or burst through when an opening presented itself or fasten on a stray ball, played to his reputation"; "Quinn's bustling bolts and maxim shooting"; "Quinn's thrilling runs and maxim shooting"; "notably centre Quinn who almost beat the [sic] Clyde himself. His heading on was valiant, and his shooting was deadly... not since he beat Rangers all alone with his three goals in the Scottish final of 1904 has the Celts' centre played a more brilliant or effective game. His first goal after a run in which he beat and baffled the entire Clyde defence, was one of his masterliest efforts". "Quinn can get goals where other centres fail. It was one of his really clever and essentially characteristic efforts that gave the winners the first goal... no centre going equals the Celt in holding on to the ball when pressed and getting in a shot by hook or by crook under great impediments."'

Of these two men, Maley, being his manager, certainly did see Quinn in action, and Handley may have. If he didn't, then he certainly talked to and knew well many who did. Their opinion is worth listening to. Handley does have points where his paranoid bias shows, for example when he compares the gentlemen of the Fourth Estate to 'the ranks of Tuscany', as if they were against him. This is not true, for newspapers like

The Scotsman, the *Glasgow Herald* and the *Daily Mail* may not have liked Celtic, but they seldom gave anything other than the highest of praise for Jimmy Quinn. Handley, otherwise known as Brother Clare, is nevertheless a fine and accurate, if occasionally romantic, Celtic historian.

It is finally worth considering what Quinn did for his native village of Croy. The scene was a 'rest camp' as it was euphemistically called in Cairo during the Second World War. It was for soldiers who had battle fatigue or were suffering from shellshock or some other form of psychiatric disturbance. One Scottish soldier had clearly seen some dreadful things at El Alamein and elsewhere and was so introverted that the medical officers feared some permanent brain damage. Another Scottish soldier was summoned and asked to talk to this chap to see if he could get through to him. This other Scotsman was a cheery fellow from the east coast, who knew his football.

He walked up to the disturbed fellow and asked him if he wanted a beer. No response. He tried again, this time asking him where he came from. Again no response. 'Glasgow?' No reply. 'Edinburgh?' No reply. He tried everyplace in Scotland he could think of before the poor fellow reluctantly said 'Croy'. 'Ah, Jimmy Quinn!' The fellow smiled, the ice broke, the two men started to talk about what they both really loved, namely Scottish football and Glasgow Celtic, and the medical men were delighted to see an improvement in the man's condition within a few days.

Croy is probably most famous now for its railway station. Any day will see large amounts of cars in the station car park where commuters have abandoned their vehicles for the day in order to go to Glasgow. Coal mining is now, of course, almost extinct, thanks to the brutal internecine disputes between Margaret Thatcher and Arthur Scargill of the 1980s. There is an RC church, a public house (which the RC church tried for a long time to keep out of the village), a recently built Miners' Welfare, a few shops and little else. But it will always be known as the birthplace of Jimmy Quinn.

Although there is now a stone, a Celtic Cross, to mark Jimmy's grave in Kilsyth Cemetery, it is a matter of some sadness that there is no obvious plaque or stone to mark the great man in the village of Croy itself. Such a thing would indeed enhance the village and no doubt please its friendly, helpful inhabitants – especially in the early years of the twenty-first century when their team is doing so well. It might even be an idea to consider the idea of changing the name of the village from 'Croy' to 'Quinn'…

The modest Jimmy would have been embarrassed by that, for he did not seek much out of the game of football. What Jimmy Quinn earned was absolutely minimal in comparison with what is earned by many lesser players a hundred years later, but he would still, without any great shadow of doubt, in 1914 have been one of the richest men in Croy. Not that it would have bothered him, for to his dying day he considered himself to be a Croy miner, as indeed he was.

Other titles published by Tempus

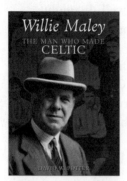

Willie Maley The Man Who Made Celtic
DAVID POTTER

Celtic owe almost everything to Willie Maley. He played in their first ever game in 1888 and won Scottish caps in 1893, before becoming Celtic's manager in 1897. He then set about building Celtic into the best team in Scotland and, from the beginning, envisaged the club as a powerful presence in world football – playing games in England, Europe and the US. As the song said, he was the man who put the 'tick' in Celtic.
0 7524 3229 X

Bobby Collins The Wee Barra
DAVID SAFFER

Bobby Collins is one of *the* great Celtic players since the Second World War. Following a remarkable 117 goals in 320 games for the Bhoys (having made his debut against Rangers in 1949), he transferred to Everton in 1958. Having made himself a firm favourite with the Goodison faithful, he moved to Leeds in 1962, again making a significant contribution to the club. Besides his excellent club career he was also capped 22 times for Scotland and led the national side. This book chronicles the career of this great player.
0 7524 3176 5

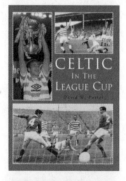

Celtic in the League Cup
DAVID POTTER

Having failed to make any real impact on the tournament for its first ten years as a peacetime competition, Celtic have subsequently made up for lost time and captured the trophy on twelve glorious occasions since 1956. Lavishly illustrated, this book is an essential purchase for anyone with an interest in the club and its history.
0 7524 2435 1

Wizards and Bravehearts A History of the Scottish National Side
DAVID POTTER

The history of Scotland's national football team from 1872 is full of highs and lows, thrill and heartbreaks, passion and pride. Read the stories of Scotland – including the 1920s when they were indubitably the best in the world and the many epic battles against the Auld Enemy. Featuring the heroes of yesteryear such as Wattie Arnott, Jimmy Quinn and Kenny Dalglish through to Jamie McFadden and Darren Fletcher, it is a must for every Scottish fan.
0 7524 3183 8

If you are interested in purchasing other books published by Tempus, or in case you have difficulty finding any Tempus books in your local bookshop, you can also place orders directly through our website
www.tempus-publishing.com